# Praise for *To Be Brave*

"McGray's heartfelt and compact memoir offers many wonderful stories. . . . Vivid, colorful tales of her grandparents' farm, some roughhousing neighborhood boys, and the trauma of her aunt's trial all add up to a greater whole, one that is relatable and optimistic. A warmhearted, concise, and compassionate account that confronts difficult issues and celebrates success."

—*Kirkus Reviews*

"With nearly cinematic drama, *To Be Brave* reconstructs the story of Karla McGray's Aunt Lila, acquitted in the 1950s for the murder of her husband following years of domestic abuse. But the power of this memoir resides in what came *before* and *after*. The legacy of violence kept secret, of fear and abuse unspoken. A teenager at the time of the trial, McGray, like all those affected by family violence, was tasked with resisting its inheritance, and the focus of this redemptive memoir is on grace. On the ordinary angels who enabled McGray to transform a terrible knowledge into a life lived out in love. We are the beneficiaries of Karla McGray's determination to deepen the decision of what it means to be brave."

—Patricia Weaver Francisco, author of
*Telling: A Memoir of Rape and Recovery*

D1469034

"*To Be Brave* is a deeply personal, educational, and spiritual story of domestic violence and sexual abuse. Karla's story opens our minds and hearts to how every abused woman is fighting to survive. This heart-wrenching story is a message of hope, resilience, and strength. Karla's courage to uncover her family's history of abuse is an inspiration to all abused women to take their first step, however small, in beginning their own heroic journey. That is—to be brave."

—Suzy Whelan, former SafeJourney program manager,
North Memorial Health

"With painful honesty, Karla lays bare the horrors of domestic violence, but shows the link between those horrors and secrecy about them. However, she reveals sacraments, the ordinary moments, that nourish us and provide vivid vistas of grace to give us hope."

—Bill Percy, PhD, psychologist emeritus

"Karla knows what she is talking about. *To Be Brave* painfully exposes the paralyzing secret of domestic violence and sexual abuse. She clarifies the legitimacy of victims' profound isolation, hopelessness, and terror. Under the real threat of violence, they must even attempt to deceive those of us who desperately want to help. This at times emotionally excruciating story of three abused women also offers hope as they discover their agency and find support for recovery and possibly even peace."

—Mark Berg, former Emergency Department
physician, North Memorial Health

# To Be Brave

*A Memoir of Domestic Violence, Resistance, and Healing*

## Karla McGray

Little
Pine
Press

Minneapolis

*To Be Brave: A Memoir of Domestic Violence, Resistance, and Healing*
Published by Little Pine Press, Minneapolis.

Print ISBN: 978-0-578-88614-5
E-book ISBN: 978-0-578-88615-2
Library of Congress Control Number 2021905985

Author photo by Judy Griesedieck
Cover design by Christian Storm
Page design by Beth Wright, Wright for Writers LLC

The author is available for book readings and
speaking engagements. Contact her via email:
tobebrave427@gmail.com

*To my mother, with gratitude for her bravery*

# Contents

❦ ❦

## Part 4: My Choice: Getting from There to Here

# Prologue

Children are powerless, and in different situations they are victims of every sorrow and mischance and rage around them, for children feel these things but without any of the ability that adults have to change them. Whatever takes a child beyond such circumstances, therefore, is an alleviation and a blessing.

—Mary Oliver, *Upstream: Selected Essays*

I did not know my mother was brave. I simply knew she was all I had. As a small child, I watched my mother carefully, searching her for myself. I was too young to read, so I read her before words were mine. I read her to see if I was good in her eyes. I read her to learn if the day would be okay, if we would be okay. I read her to learn if that day she had time to pay attention to me, or if work would pull her away. I read her to learn if I was a valued, loved being in this world.

I learned early how to watch, how to see: the small signs of weight in the folds above my mother's eyes, on the corners of her mouth, as she carried both of us. I learned to watch her hands shake or watch her face for signs of fear. In my mother's younger years it was as if we lived in a sea of tall grass, buffeted by the wild winds of her choices, tossed here and there with her pursuit of security, her struggle to survive, her determination to save us both. We were both on high alert, ever vigilant because we had to be, she for me and me learning from her.

I did not know the women in my family were brave. She was my mother. These were my aunts and my grandmother. They were my family, women seeking to get by one more day, to love, live, laugh as often as possible. As a child, I only knew the aftershock of their traumas, the way fear and upheaval became normal.

There was rage, mischance, and sorrow to be sure, but as Mary Oliver writes, "whatever takes a child beyond such circumstances, therefore, is an alleviation and a blessing." These women in my life brought all their rage, mischance, and sorrow into my life, but they also brought alleviation and blessing.

My mother's story does not stand alone, nor does mine. There isn't one story. One woman's story impacts another woman's story, then another and another. This is what I learned when, by choice, I revisited what I knew of the stories of the women in my family.

I never intended to write this story, though I carried it inside me for years. I held it inside until one evening I set it free in a few words that became part of a prayer. It floated above a ballroom at a benefit dinner for victims of domestic violence. A woman in the room recognized the brief details and took it down deep in her heart, then offered it back to me wrapped in more details. Her revelation struck chords of memory and pain I thought I had successfully buried. With time, I knew I had to talk with her to know more. With more time, I learned members of my family wanted this story honored as well.

This story begins in Garrison, a 1.1-square-mile town of 210 people on the west side of Mille Lacs Lake in Crow Wing County, Minnesota. You could easily miss this drive-by town unless you stopped to eat at the Blue Goose Restaurant and Bar or refuel at the Y gas station, named for the junction of Highway 169 and County Road 6. A fifteen-foot-tall statue of a walleye stands on the shore of the lake to greet cabin owners, fishermen, and tourists, reminding visitors there is a town here, a town that holds lives and stories.

The name *Garrison* is derived from the French verb *garir*, which means "to defend, protect." In 1959 Garrison became the embodied fortress for one woman, my aunt Lila, as she sought to defend and protect the one thing she loved most in this world—her child. To grasp the garrison a woman will become to protect her child, you need to know the deep-down inside of her: the chambers of her heart pulsing beat by beat with love learned in her family, the underside of her skin that feels pain through its cells down to the bone when it is beaten, the cortex of her brain that kicks in on high alert when danger is approaching. If necessary she will deploy every raw nerve of her interior militia and station it—ready—as the enemy encroaches on the safety barrier she has created for herself and her child. She will do whatever it takes to protect her child, even at the risk of her own life.

These events had not been discussed in my family for over fifty-five years when I began asking questions. The first recovered thread of this story was handed to me at that benefit dinner, and once I discovered it, I began to see how the threads of three women's lives wove together—my aunt Lila; my mother, Millie; and me.

When I began writing, I thought I was going to tell my aunt Lila's story: her experience of being a battered woman, the impact this had on her young life, and the shocking stand she took to protect herself and her child. As I researched, I began to understand the parallels with my own mother's experience. I kept tugging and pulling out the details and realized I was at the center of these interwoven threads. There was no way I could tell their stories without telling my own.

As I researched and wrote, I began to see that a woman doesn't stand alone. She lives in a web of relationships beginning with her family, but most especially with her children. We, the children, land in the arms of our mothers and begin to learn what it means to be in a relationship. That start isn't always poetic, romantic, perfect, or well-timed. It can be messy. As afterbirth clings to a newborn baby, so might the complexity of a mother's life cling to her child. It can take a lifetime to wipe it away.

Parts of my mother's story were mostly a mystery to me. After she died in 1975, I found clues about her early life in her papers, the detritus in her closets and boxes, but she was no longer available to answer my questions. As a child, I had learned quickly that my questions landed on her as if on a hot stove. They burned, so I learned to pull back, not ask. The answers were too close, too intense with the heat of memory. I had no awareness of the cloak of stigma my mother wore as a young woman. Like my mother,

I also learned at a very early age not to tell my own secrets. My secrets were dangerous. I had been told people would get hurt if I told these secrets, even to my mother—most especially to my mother.

Lila died in 2007. While she lived, she set boundaries around her story by never discussing it, just as my mother put walls around her past. As a family, we learned the signals, paid attention to them, and stayed behind the yellow tape that said "crime scene." Such boundaries are powerful, have authority, and are difficult to cross. I don't believe my family wanted to revisit the terror experienced by my mother, then Lila, and later our entire family. Touching the raw wounds might make them bleed again.

Our family went through these traumas in the 1950s. It wasn't an era of therapy, processing experiences, or feelings. Everyone bucked up, tried to stay strong for each other, moved on, and got back to the hard work of everyday farm life. My family moved through these nightmares, and when they were over, a silence settled in. It was heavy, like soft cement, filling in every corner around the stories. Then it hardened, and these stories became impermeable secrets.

I hope that by telling these stories, I will empower other mothers and fathers to be honest with their own children. Healing is only possible through shedding stigmas, secrets, and shame. Adults in families make mistakes. Being powerless, children may absorb these mistakes and decide they themselves are the problem. I hope this story empowers grown children to tell their experience of their parents' mistakes and how it shaped their own lives.

As far as I know, I was the only child in our extended family who experienced domestic violence and sexual abuse at a young age. My mother chose to live with an abusive man for five years. She did not know he sexually abused me when she left me alone with him while she worked. She did not know he threatened to hurt her if I told. After we escaped him, I lived alone with my mother and was wary and suspicious of all men. Then, when I was thirteen years old, Lila shot and killed her violent husband. This occurred when I was struggling to discern what it means to be female in a world with men in charge. I was deeply shaken by what happened. Despite having witnessed violence in my own life as a little girl, murder was incomprehensible to me.

In both instances, through my mother's escape and Lila's trial, the adults around me were traumatized, in shock, but got busy doing what needed to be done. The family sheltered my mother and put together resources for Lila's legal defense. I was loved, but left on my own to understand how to make sense of these events and what meaning they might have in my future.

I have told this story as honestly as I can. Many details died with Lila and my mother, members of our family, or the legal community. I have gathered the details that exist in historical records. Family members were bravely willing to bear witness to stories they'd kept silent for fifty-five years. I have had to imagine some thoughts, moments, and experiences of those no longer living based on my relationship with them or on stories I have heard or researched. However, the reality was probably much worse than anything described here.

In 2013, as I began putting these words on paper, five young women went missing in the Twin Cities area. All five were suspected to have been victims of domestic violence. It was believed these women were beaten, then murdered, by the men in their lives. This story of men viewing women as property to do with as they please has gone on since the beginning of time.

As I wrote, volunteers were walking through marshes, riverbeds, and prairies, one step at a time, searching for the missing five. I felt a connection between these young women, my mother, my aunt Lila, and me. I wished that by now things would be different, that some progress would have been made. Eventually, each of their bodies was found and the suspicion of domestic violence proved to be true. In 2019, 1,527 women in the United States were killed by male intimate partners. Most were killed with firearms. An abuser's access to a firearm increases the risk of femicide by 500 percent.

In my research, I contacted the Crow Wing County Judicial Center, the University of Minnesota Law Library, the Hennepin County Law Library, and the Minnesota Coalition for Battered Women (now Violence Free Minnesota). I discovered that records of murders in domestic violence cases have been retained only since 1988. If a woman kills her abuser, an acquittal is rare. However, I learned that in acquittals of any kind, charges are dismissed and no transcripts of trial proceedings are kept. In a conviction or acquittal, all cases are given a case file number. The case file may be kept in the local county for a time, but it is later transferred to the Minnesota History Center archives. Years later, with the case file number it is possible to recover details of a trial—more details if there is a conviction. Yet even with a case file number, I discovered it is difficult to learn how many women have been convicted of killing their abusive spouses or partners.

With the help of the Minnesota History Center staff, I located my aunt Lila's case file and newspaper articles. This file was the beginning of unearthing a story that held chunks of silence, hardened secrets, and packed-down pain, all adding to the weight of my family's long-carried sadness. I interviewed my family members, as well as family members of participants in my aunt's trial. I corresponded with my mother's best friend, who is now in her nineties and has clear memories of their time working together in Seattle during World War II. She filled in gaps and details of the war years and my mother's life as only a dear friend can, with love and compassion for a woman's reality during that time.

This is the story of three women, but it is also the story of every woman who has looked into the eyes of a man who has a death grip on her throat and holds her life in his hands. It is the story of every woman who sees a fist coming at her, ready to deliver bruises and split skin. The story of the grit it takes to survive each and every day. The story of every child who witnesses violence or experiences it directly. The story of a family that takes the harm done to its loved ones into its core, resulting in reverberations over decades. The story of what it takes for a woman to heal from a legacy of violence.

My mother, my aunt, and I each healed in our own way, within our own historical context, with the resources available to us. The tenor and social awareness of the times made all the difference, but the essential strand of these stories is how we resurrected ourselves, began life over again, and strived to heal.

**Part 1**

# Independence Day

Owning our stories and loving ourselves through the process is the bravest thing we will ever do.

—Brené Brown

# 1

# July 4, 1959

Spending the Fourth of July holiday weekend up north on the family farm was a time my mother and I looked forward to each year. It was a relief to get out of Minneapolis and our small, hot apartment. After the holiday weekend was over, I usually remained on the farm for the rest of the summer. We didn't own a car, so frequently we rode the bus, but that year Harold, my mother's friend from work, offered to drive us. The route took us past my aunt Lila's house outside Garrison, so we stopped to visit her; her husband, John; and their adopted eighteen-month-old baby. They lived in a rundown trailer that had been sided to look like a house.

It wasn't a happy visit. Something was wrong. Lila wore sunglasses even though it was early evening. There were hushed conversations in the kitchen between Lila and my mother. I played with the baby, pretending not to listen, but I could tell my mother was upset. We didn't stay long. My mother seemed anxious to get to the farm. In the car, I remember my mother talking with Harold about her concerns for Lila. She was anxious to talk to my grandfather about what she had seen.

After we left, based on later accounts, this is what happened. This story is reconstructed, narrated, and imagined from stories shared in our family and newspaper coverage.

*Lila went back into the house after waving goodbye to Millie, Karla, and Harold. She went into the baby's room, stood by the side of the crib, and looked down at her sleeping baby boy. In the dark, she could smell his milky breath and the scent of baby powder. She reached down, laid her hand softly on his back, and felt his chest rise and fall.*

*This was life beneath the palm of her hand. Life. This was the center of her world right here, right now. She needed time to think.*

*She stepped out through the screen door into the humid summer night. She couldn't sleep. Her mind was too busy, her heart too heavy. Her body trembled. The image of the shotgun standing in the corner of her kitchen accompanied her as she stepped into the night air. She was no stranger to guns. She had been deer hunting with her family since she was a young girl. Hunting was a way of life on the farm, but this gun was different. She and her child were its prey.*

*She needed to feel held, comforted. The humid darkness surprised her as it embraced her, held her close, and pulled in her frayed edges. The compassion of the night moved her, and she found herself turning her bruised face upward. Looking at the vast night sky, she felt very small. She saw shimmering stars, but their beauty was too painful to take in just now. She could feel tears stinging the corners of her eyes.*

*Millie had noticed her bruises. There were questions, too many questions. In the six months since moving back to Minnesota, Lila had hidden the beatings from her family. She was worried Millie would tell Daddy and Mom. She feared what Daddy might do if he discovered John had been beating her for years.*

*She listened to the loud drone of the cicadas off in the marsh behind the house. This night, the sound was different. It sounded like old women keening, wailing. She listened over the lament for the sound of her baby stirring in his sleep, but he was quiet. She was all alone with her own heartbeat and her thoughts.*

*John had lost his job at the Y Club, which made him even angrier these days. These last weeks had been rougher than usual. Any little thing seemed to set him off in a rage. He had loaded his shotgun and, each night, set it down on the kitchen table at dinner. As he drank and ranted at her about things she hadn't done around the house or any sound the baby made, he waved the gun around. Then he aimed it at her. Most terrifyingly, he aimed it at the baby.*

*As she stood there in the darkness, her heart raced as she remembered watching that gun aimed at her son. Then she heard something—not something outside in the dark, but a sound that rose up inside herself, a primordial beat in pace with her own, a drum of life calling her to live, whatever the cost. It filled her head, her entire body, throbbing and getting louder and louder.*

*The sound of a car in the distance broke through the roar inside her. The bars in Garrison were closed by now. She could make out John's headlights in the distance, tiny pinpricks getting larger and larger by the minute. The headlights were weaving from one side of the road to the other. He was drunk again. She turned back toward* the house with an impulse that had no reason, no brakes. As she opened the door to the house, she heard the tires of the car turning onto the gravel driveway. The drumbeat roared within her as she reached for John's loaded shotgun standing in the corner by the kitchen table. This time, when she stepped back outside into the thick night air, it held her up, held her strong, to give her courage for what came next.

The car came to a sudden stop as John slammed on the brakes, the gravel grinding deep into the dirt, marking this moment for what it was: a man coming home drunk and not in full control. Lila could see John's shadow through the windshield, fumbling to turn the engine off and get his keys out of the ignition. It took him even longer to reach the door handle, get the car door open, and struggle out of the car.

She was shaking as she stood with the shotgun in her hands. She saw John's feet hit the ground below the car door, saw him balance himself with the door of the car, attempt to steady himself as he struggled to close the door. She couldn't see his eyes or his face, just his dark frame silhouetted against the light gravel. Slowly, he turned in her direction, and for the first time, he saw her standing by the door to the house. In a split second, Lila lifted the shotgun, aimed straight at him, and pulled the trigger. Boom! Then there was silence.

Lila stood frozen, not believing what had just happened. She saw John down on the ground. Then she realized he was pulling himself up on his hands and knees. She watched as he got one foot under his body and pushed himself up to stand. He lifted his head, looked right at her, and growled, "I am going to kill you for this!" He began to take a step toward her. In an instant she pulled the trigger and shot him a second time. She didn't know if she hit him or not, but she didn't wait to find out. In a panic, she ran into the house and lunged for the box of shotgun shells John had left lying on the kitchen counter. She threw the lid off the box, grabbing shells as they tumbled to the floor. She managed to hit the release lock, jam one shell into each chamber, and slam the shotgun back into its locked position. She raced toward the door, then stopped. She peered into the yard through the screen, scouring the darkness for any sign of movement. She saw John lying on the ground. She waited. Her heart pounded inside her head, her chest, pulsing in every sinew of her body. Only after waiting did she slowly open the screen door and step outside, holding the gun tightly. She watched. She waited, a hunter on high alert, prepared to shoot to kill. John lay there on his belly, a dark pool forming around his body.

The pool of blood was growing larger. Lila listened for the baby's cries. He hadn't wakened. There was no sound from within the house and no movement on the ground. Lila went to a back room, found an old brown blanket on the floor, and returned to the screen door. She waited again, hearing her own breath coming in gasps, her heart pounding inside her chest. Every sense in her body was acutely alert to any sign of a threat. John remained still. She slowly opened the screen door, the groan of the stretching spring a roar in the silence. It startled her. She checked one more time to be sure John hadn't moved, then approached his body with caution, terrified he might reach out and grab her. Once she was close enough, she lunged and threw the blanket over his body. She did not want to take a chance that her baby would see this horrible sight. Now she just wanted to get away from the house.

She ran into the house and hurried to the crib. Taking a deep breath to slow herself down, she gently gathered up her sleeping child in his soft cotton blanket, walked to the screen door, and opened it slowly, looking to see if anything had changed. She saw the dark blanket lying over John's body, which didn't move. It felt safe to leave, so Lila skirted his body by a wide margin as she made her way to the road to walk to the neighbors' house. As she stepped onto the road, she could feel her baby's moist head against her neck. She didn't want to look back, but she did just one last time to assure herself she wasn't being followed. Her son was a big boy, so she was grateful she didn't have far to walk. His sleepy dead weight hugged against her chest; his blond hair peeked out of the blanket. His breath punctuated her steps, fueling the determination she needed to propel herself forward. With each step she left the horror behind her. Her neighbors' house was dark as she walked up the front steps.

Lila knocked on the door, but it was a few minutes before she saw a light turn on inside the house. Lyle opened the door. His eyes widened with surprise when he saw his young neighbor standing on his steps holding her baby.

She looked at Lyle and said, "I shot John. I need to call the sheriff."

"Oh my God." Lyle quickly hustled her into the house.

Lila made two calls, first to the sheriff, then to her parents' farm. She informed the sheriff that she had shot her husband. She informed my uncle Sidney, "I shot John. Come get the baby."

# 2

# SafeJourney

*November 2007*

"Did this incident in your family happen in Garrison, Minnesota?"

I turned to see a woman squatting by my chair. Her face was framed by wavy brown hair. She had soft brown eyes. I was shocked. "Yes! What? How did you know?" I was trying to keep my voice down. I had just sat down after giving the invocation prayer, which I had done for many years as a chaplain, at the benefit dinner for SafeJourney, the program at North Memorial Hospital for domestic violence victims.

She responded quietly, "My father was the one who arrested your aunt. He was the Crow Wing County sheriff at the time."

I gasped. I was stunned. "I can't believe this. I need to talk with you."

"My name is Allyn. You can reach me through my husband, Tom, at the hospital. He's the medical director."

My eyes filled with tears. It was all I could do to utter, "Thank you," as I tried to keep my composure. I looked around at the other women at my table. They were all engaged in conversations with one another. I was in such a state of shock I couldn't tell them what had just happened.

I first learned about SafeJourney when I began my work as a chaplain resident at North Memorial Hospital in Robbinsdale, Minnesota. The program supports victims of domestic violence, trains emergency department staff and physicians to identify symptoms of abuse, and has advocates on call twenty-four hours a day to provide support and resources to individuals who have been beaten by their spouses or partners. As soon as I learned about it, I wanted to do what I could to help, but I had never told my colleagues why. That evening, I had decided to break my silence.

I prefaced the invocation with these words: "Each of us here this evening has a personal reason why we support SafeJourney. Some of us have been victims of domestic violence, while others have loved ones who have been victims. My aunt, at the age of twenty-six, shot and killed her abusive husband. She was charged with murder. It was a devastating experience for my family." Sitting in another part of the room, Allyn had listened to this brief summary, recognized the facts, and realized she might have a connection to this story.

Lila had died on September 19, 2007, two months prior to the benefit. I officiated her funeral at the Koop Funeral Home in Crosby, Minnesota, surrounded by my mother's side of the family, which included my remaining living aunts, uncles, and cousins. As I gave her eulogy, I was hesitant and skirted around the tragic experiences in her young life. I spoke of her courage but did not describe details of her story. No one else in the family, not one person, stood up that day to speak about what Lila had endured.

It was as if this family memory had been wiped clean, but we all knew it was there. We simply kept the boundaries Lila had imposed on her story. She never talked about what happened, and neither did we, not even after her death. I was complicit in the silence. As a child and young adult, I took my cues from other members of my family. My mother never discussed it with me, nor I with her, because it might mean revisiting our own past.

# 3

## An Appearance Story

### *2009*

Over a year had passed since the SafeJourney benefit dinner. I felt resistance about contacting Allyn. My gut tightened with fear at the mere thought of making the call, feelings that stemmed from my own early childhood experiences. I kept remembering Allyn's face and words. It was a miracle that she had appeared out of the crowd, but I felt uneasy. We had not discussed this story in my family for so many years. I wasn't sure I wanted to reopen those memories, but as of that instant at that benefit dinner, the memories were already opened. Therapy and spiritual direction had taught me there was no going back. It was time.

I phoned Allyn's husband, Tom, to get her contact information. As soon as she heard my voice, she assured me this was a welcome phone call, and we scheduled lunch for the following week.

When she arrived at the restaurant, she was warm and gracious, which helped me immediately feel at ease. She brought along a folder filled with newspaper articles, photos, and memorabilia from her father's life and career. Over lunch she shared with me her memories of my aunt Lila. She had photos of herself and her sister, Karen, taken during the years the family resided in the old brick house in Brainerd that served as the county jail. She told me how she and her sister celebrated "Jailhouse Rock"–themed birthday parties, maximizing their unique living arrangement.

Then she looked me right in the eyes and said, "My father always said your aunt's case was the worst he ever had to deal with in his time as sheriff." Her father experienced a lot of sleepless nights and likely dealt with post-traumatic stress from his work, though there weren't words for it at the time. He died at age fifty-one, three years after my aunt's trial. He sat down in his favorite chair to have a cup of coffee and died of a coronary occlusion. His wife was left alone with their three children. "My mother told me she could never meet another man like my dad. There was nobody like him." Allyn looked wistful as she told me about her mother's love for her father and then shared her advice: "She told me to pick a man that you respect and you'll never be sorry."

She went on to tell me about those challenging years following her father's death. The family was allowed to live in the jailhouse until they found a home to rent in Brainerd. They were the last to use the jail as a residence. Her mother bought a gift shop that helped support the family. She lived to be eighty-five years old and never remarried. Allyn's eyes lit up as she recalled that the man who'd succeeded her dad in the job had said her dad was "the best sheriff he had ever met."

Then she turned to Lila's story again, as if recalling why we were meeting. "Karen and I would make breakfast for the prisoners. I delivered food to your aunt when she was in jail." The woman sitting before me had been that close to my aunt on that dark morning after her arrest. Allyn said again, "Yes, my father always said your aunt's case was one of the worst cases he ever had to deal with."

When Allyn spoke to me at the benefit dinner, she opened the door to this story. There was no closing it again. At the time I had no idea where it was going to take me because it meant crossing the threshold of many other stories. Unknowingly, she was the instrument of grace that ignited my desire to learn as much as possible about my past, confront it, and struggle with it. She asked a single question that pierced fear and penetrated boundaries imposed from the grave—not only Lila's, but also my mother's.

# 4

## Stairway to Heaven

### *2013*

"A story like that stays with you," my uncle Sidney said in a whisper, staring me right in the eye. I had asked him about Lila's trial. In that moment, he and I were all alone, suspended in his words, despite standing on a deck in bright sunshine with family members milling all around us.

I had been nervous about asking Sidney what he remembered about Lila's legal case and trial. He was eighteen years old at that time. To my knowledge, no one had spoken about it in years. They seemed to have placed these painful memories high on a shelf in a dark closet, and no one wanted to take them down. If so, there were other memories on that shelf as well.

I had not spent time with my extended family for years. Yet here I was, just outside Princeton, Minnesota, attending a memorial gathering for Anna, my cousin's wife. Anna had died at a young age from cancer. I stood on the deck surrounded by cousins, aunts, and uncles—now older, white-haired men and women. Many of them lived in northern Minnesota or in other states; I lived in the Twin Cities. Perhaps we justified our lack of contact by being wrapped up in our own families' lives, work, challenges, and losses over the years. Perhaps I was the only one who had been out of contact.

Deep down I knew there was more to it for me—a reason for my distance. I knew that resentment and old anger hung like cobwebs on my heart. Over the years, my mother had helped her siblings many times.

She supported them financially, provided housing, and gave encouragement through divorces and job losses. Then, at age forty-three, my mother needed open-heart surgery. She was in the hospital, and I was in a bind. I was twenty-two years old, alone, and feeling desperate. I needed to move my mother out of her apartment immediately and sell her car. I needed a decent-paying job to augment our income, even though I was a full-time student at the University of Minnesota. I called up north to our family for help. When no one called me back, I was hurt and angry. I called the family again, and this time, I essentially ordered them to arrive on a particular day with a trailer to help me pack up my mother's apartment. They showed up.

When my mother died seven years later, a small memorial service was held. I was twenty-nine years old, grief-stricken, and lost, and I didn't know what to do. My grandparents and extended family traveled to the city to attend the service, but left the same afternoon and returned to the farm. No one in the family remained to support me. Later, I cleaned out my mother's apartment alone. I never forgot.

From my view now, I realize my aunts and uncles were no doubt worried about my grandparents. There were also things to attend to on the farm. But in my young mind and heart, I held on to that perceived lack of support, and it hurt, so I kept my distance, staying in touch primarily with my grandparents. Over the years, I heard rumors about conflicts in the family. I didn't need the family politics. It was easier being solo. I had been on my own at a young age and knew that role well.

At Anna's memorial, I stepped back into the family. I came with questions and hoped for some answers. I was an older woman with a deeper understanding of forgiveness. We had all been brought to our knees by life's blows, me included. Now we were all older individuals, more accepting of others and ourselves. There were no pretenses about who we were or the lives we had lived.

At some deep level, I longed to be a part of their lives again. Of the seven children in my mother's family, four remained. The three oldest daughters were gone: Lila, Bernice, and my mother, Millie, who would have turned eighty years old that April. I imagined standing on the deck with her; she would have been a white-haired woman, wrinkled from too many years of smoking, like these older family members with familiar features buried inside folds of loose skin. I felt I was my mother at this gathering—her embodied presence.

Our conversation had quieted down, so in my discomfort I broke the silence. "I told you that I scattered Mom's ashes on the farm, didn't I? Along the top of that hill on the far side of the pasture." Everyone looked at me but didn't say anything. I didn't know how to read their silence. "She was most at home, most at peace, on the farm. It just seemed natural that was where she would want to be." More silence. Now feeling even more uncomfortable, I babbled on. "The day I scattered Mom's ashes, I walked along that hilltop over beyond the windmill with her ashes in my backpack. I remember a breeze was blowing. Then suddenly, a doe came out of the woods. I was upwind of her, so she didn't smell me. I watched her as she loped through the meadow. Then she stopped and cocked her ears. She was copper brown and beautiful." My aunt and uncle listened to my story—Della with a wisp of a smile on her face, Sidney looking pensive, both no doubt picturing that familiar meadow. "Then she just kept going, trotting along, stopping to graze now and then. It was weird. It felt like a visit from my mother. It made the moment so beautiful. I knew it was her trying to tell me it'd all be okay." My aunt and uncles stood there, transfixed. I realized I had gotten lost in my story. "I had other visits from my mother."

"What visits? You never told us about that." It was as if Della had awakened from a trance.

My mother was the oldest child in the family. She was a rudder among her siblings, steering their lives as they grew up, providing safe harbor in our home when they couldn't keep sailing on their own. They moved in with us, sometimes bringing their whole families. Something shifted in our family when my mother died. My grandfather never recovered. My grandmother sewed the seams of the family together the best she could after losing a child. But with my mother's sudden death, our family understood the fragility of life.

I stood with my aunt and uncle, the sunlight shining on my own head of white hair, my own wrinkles. I knew I was my mother's legacy at this gathering.

"You know, as you've gotten older, you look more and more like your mother. She was always really pretty," Della said out of the blue. Just as I'd thought: they were looking at me and thinking of her. I laughed, feeling a bit awkward about her compliment. Then she added, "Of course, we never really knew exactly what color her hair was, since she always colored it." We all laughed. I loved Della's wry humor and her way of lightening difficult moments. "But in photos I've seen when she was young, she looked just like Rita Hayworth."

The moment turned quiet again, as each of us seemed to be remembering a sweeter time in our family. Now one of the children's children had lost his young wife to cancer. Anna was a woman who loved angels, and her early death was a reminder that no one can be protected. Here in the sunlight, in the first real warmth of spring, we overlooked a garden that had at its center a metal spiral staircase that climbed up into the open air, pointing toward the clear blue sky. At its base, a bed of copper mulch held colorful flowers and angels. Anna called it her "stairway to heaven."

Unspoken words hung in the bright heat of the sun like butterflies too hot to fly. Missing parents and grandparents, missing sisters, tragedies, regrets, secrets, grief, jokes, and laughter around the farmhouse kitchen table. The farmland was now a scattering garden, and a cemetery north of Ross Lake Township in the town of Emily, where my grandparents' headstones turned gray with age, had become our family's sacred place.

The moment was thick with memories. Then it slipped away into getting another beverage, a helping of food, or saying goodbye. We all sensed there would be another time when we would be remembering together again, when another dear one would be missing.

Standing alone for a moment with my uncle Sidney, I decided to take a risk, knowing I might catch him by surprise. I said tentatively, "Sidney, I've been looking back into Lila's case." Sidney's eyes widened, and he glanced at me with surprise. "I just wanted to know more about that incident in our family. I found some articles in old newspapers."

Now he turned his face directly toward mine. "Where did you find them?"

I really had his attention. "At the Minnesota History Center in St. Paul. Do you by chance remember the names of any of the people involved in her trial?"

"Sure, like it was yesterday." For a moment he was suspended in a flashback. "Joe Ryan was her lawyer. Carl Erickson was the prosecutor. Al Krueger was the sheriff. Galarneault was the judge." Sidney rattled off these names as if he had been waiting for someone to ask the question for a long time.

"My God, you remember a lot."

"Yes, a story like that stays with you," he whispered.

$$\overline{5}$$

# Palm Sunday

## *2014*

I left my house at 7:00 a.m. to drive two hours north from Minneapolis, past Onamia, through the small town of Garrison on the shores of Mille Lacs Lake, and on to Brainerd. I had done more research and writing on my aunt Lila's case. My work as a full-time chaplain in a Level I trauma center was demanding, so I fit in writing my family story whenever I could find time. But I needed to prepare myself to dig deeper. This was the day I would interview Della and Sidney, my mother's youngest siblings, about their memories of Lila, the murder, and the trial. I had no idea what to expect but was grateful they were willing to meet with me. I felt anticipation and anxiety simultaneously.

It was a gray April morning. The temperature was a little above freezing. It was a perfect morning to nestle in for a long drive with a good cup of hot coffee and *Weekend Edition* on Minnesota Public Radio. As I headed west up I-94, I thought about missing Palm Sunday, the first day of Holy Week. I was sorry not to see the children's procession into church.

I thought about how this day is also known as Passion Sunday, the word *passion* coming from the Latin noun *passio*, meaning suffering. When I had spoken with Della on the telephone, she began to cry. My upbeat, always-cracking-a-joke aunt began remembering. "It's hard to go back to those days."

On this day in the first century, a man rode on a donkey into Jerusalem to fly in the face of systems that inflicted violent injustice on peasants like him. As the leafless landscape flew by, I thought about the implications of Lila taking control and rising up against the violence she had lived with for seven years: for her, in that moment, the only way.

The landscape was bland and beige. The farm fields had been turned over in the fall, waiting to be planted in the spring. The old two-lane highway was now four lanes as I flew past Elk River with no glimpse of the town. Modest houses lined the highway, ATVs and pickup trucks adorned with monster wheels in their yards. A billboard boasting "Dancers and Booze: Need We Say More?" was positioned just in front of the billboard for the Faith Christian School. Before I realized it, I had passed Princeton and Milaca. Since the freeway skirted these once familiar little towns, I realized I'd have to take a detour if I wanted a piece of pie in a local café.

A story came on the radio about Corey, a young soldier who, along with his father, was a guest of President Barack Obama at the State of the Union Address. Injured by an IED in Iraq, the soldier had spent three months in a coma and many months in rehab. As I listened, I thought that if there was a contemporary passion story, this was it. As members of Congress gave Corey a standing ovation for several minutes, his father turned to him and said, "This is for you." Corey replied, "This is not about me, but a larger story." This reminded me that Lila's story was a much larger story. I was on my way to find out all I could learn.

As I approached Onamia, a sign announced, "Bird Houses, Bird Feeders, Treasures of Old: Worth Stopping." I saw Mille Lacs Lake come into view and a sign reading "Wig Wam Bay." I remembered how, as a child, it was always a treat to see this vast lake appear. There was no giant casino in my childhood, but little resorts still cropped up along the highway. The empty ice houses now lining the road had held beer parties, fishing lines, and small televisions last winter. Covered boats waited alongside empty cabins. The giant walleye statue welcomed me into Garrison.

I stopped at the gas station. The clerk at the counter inside welcomed me, "Hi there. Let me know if ya need any help." As I approached the cash register, she asked in an upbeat Midwestern manner, "Did ya find what you need? Those corporate people redid our station and took out lotsa good stuff. They told us they wanted to stock us like the stations in the Cities." Now I knew I was up north for sure.

At the Y in Garrison, I took the left fork on Highway 6, knowing that soon I would drive past Lila's former trailer, which had been converted to look like a house. The place looked different, but even after fifty-five years, it still made me shudder.

I hadn't seen Sidney and Della since Anna's memorial gathering. "Who are these three old white-haired people?" I asked as I greeted Sidney and gave him a big hug. His companion, Donna, served us coffee, brownies, carrot cupcakes, and chocolate chip cookies, and then she left the room. The hospitality let me know what my visit meant to them.

This was the moment. This was what I had hoped for several years earlier, when all I could feel was fear and reluctance about approaching my family to share what they knew about Lila's story. I was deeply moved by the image of the three of us, a trinity of family, sitting at a wooden kitchen table, breaking brownies together. We sat in awkward silence for a moment.

"I can't tell you what it means to me to be here," I said, choking back tears. "I am not sure where to begin. I thought we might look at a timeline of events to get us started. It might jog some memories. Would that be helpful?" I had prepared Lila's story from Independence Day, when she shot John, to Thanksgiving, when she went to trial.

Three children sat in the bodies of three aging adults, recalling details, memories, painful days. I tried to ask questions as gently as I could without pushing too hard. There was reverence in being able to speak about the past. We helped each other along, picking our way through stories, recalling names and sequences of events.

"Who answered the phone when Lila called?" I asked.

"I did," Sidney replied, a sober look on his face.

"Did you go to the scene with my mother?" I wanted to know every detail. Even though I was there, I couldn't remember.

Sidney filled in the gaps. "No, Harold drove her. I stayed with the folks. I was worried about them. And we still had chores to do."

"Della, where were you?"

"I was in Minneapolis. I hadn't left for the holiday weekend yet. Once Sidney called me, I hurried to get a ride home."

Going back to those hours after the shooting was hard. I handed out tissues to both of them and used one myself. At one point, I went to the bathroom, mostly to give all of us a break, take a deep breath, and absorb what I was hearing and feeling. I wondered if there were any easier way I could have done this. When I returned, there were freshly filled cups of coffee and more chocolate.

A very painful part was remembering the devastating impact on my grandparents. Sidney recalled, "Mom and Daddy were nervous wrecks. They were terrified that Lila would go to prison. We were all so worried about the baby and what would happen to him." He left the kitchen for a moment, obviously emotional.

"Is this too much to handle?" I asked Della.

"It's hard. I think we just buried all this stuff deep in our brains some-where. It's hard to bring it all back up again," she said as she wiped her nose.

When Sidney returned, I asked, "Were there good things that came out of it?"

"People sent checks to help with the legal costs. There was a fundraiser held for the family. People were worried about us. You learn who your friends and neighbors are in a situation like that." Remembering any small kindnesses brought more tears. "And there was the Greek family who owned the little restaurant near the courthouse. Unbelievable." Re-calling this made Sidney's chin tremble. His eyes filled with tears. Expres-sions of unexpected support from strangers touched the family deeply.

Four hours and many cups of coffee later, plus many tissues and trips to the bathroom, our journey through the large doorways and down the long halls of memory was over for now. We had cracked open this family story, and our hearts got wrung out.

Revisiting Lila's experience in detail brought it forward to the present with a zoom lens. We broke the tradition of keeping family secrets. The children who came after us would now know the whole story. Sidney and Della entrusting me with more details was a real act of love. At the end of our time together Sidney looked at me and said, "You need to write this story." I hugged him and Donna and tried to express my gratitude in words that felt inadequate to what had been offered.

I left with Della to go to lunch, but before we could get settled into our booth at a local restaurant, her cell phone rang. Sidney had remembered two more important details and wanted to talk to me right away. As I wrote down his additional memories, I sensed there would be more now that we'd rustled around in the dark corners of family history, taken out articles and documents from archives, and wept over the jury's decision.

Sitting in my car in the parking lot, I thanked Sidney. He replied, "It is what it is, and this story needs to be told."

He was right. Telling this story is my way, our family's way, of acknowledging the strength of women, the extraordinary faith of a family, and the long-term effects of trauma on children. To keep silent sustains the grief and pain. To keep silent allows the abuser to continue to wield power over and over again. Many women and families I have met in my work as a chaplain have endured similar trauma, horror, and pain. Telling this story lets them know they are not alone.

## Part 2

# Lila's Story

When the heart grieves over what it has lost, the spirit rejoices over what it has left.

—Sufi epigram

# 6

# The Middle Child

My aunt Lila is one of the bravest women I have ever known.

She was a small woman, quiet and gentle in her demeanor, not the kind of person you would ever imagine could kill a man. She had a wry sense of humor, loved to kid around, play practical jokes, and tell funny family stories. But after she died, as I officiated her funeral, I realized I never knew the inside-out of her. I did not know her soul, dreams, and yearnings, or the things she longed for in life.

I mostly knew the facts of her life. She had married one violent husband and two more husbands after the trial. I knew she had worked in the snowmobile manufacturing plants in small-town northern Minnesota, an area without many viable job opportunities for women. I knew she had traveled to Texas, married a man, adopted a baby, and later, killed that man. I knew the events that ensued after the shooting happened not only to her, but our family and me, a thirteen-year-old girl at the time.

I now call my aunt heroic.

Lila was born on April 23, 1933, the fourth and middle child of seven in the Palmer family. My grandmother had birthed three children by the time the Depression consumed the country. Birth control wasn't an option; abstinence and timing only worked to a point. My grandmother's sister, Norma, once said that when my grandmother mentioned not feeling well or having the flu, she figured it meant there had been another miscarriage. Norma knew two premature babies were buried on the farm. The loss of an infant was an experience women endured without much acknowledgment, but it was a challenge to keep the babies from coming.

When Lila was a toddler, my grandmother became pregnant with her fifth child. This time the pregnancy was different. My grandmother was severely ill throughout it. My uncle Dale was born on September 20, 1937, with early indications that something wasn't normal. Developmentally, Dale progressed differently than the other children. The differences were subtle at first, but it became more obvious when it was time for Dale to go to school. My grandmother told me she and my grandfather were encouraged by a doctor to place Dale in an institution that housed children with cognitive disabilities. My grandfather was outraged and indignantly told the doctor he and my grandmother would take their son home, love him, and raise him on the farm with the rest of their children. Dale became a special child in our family. He worked on the farm and taught every grandchild how to clean barns, chop wood, and carry water.

The challenging pregnancy, delivery, and baby left Lila to fend for herself as my grandmother cared for Dale. As is often the case, the oldest child, my mother, was the one Lila turned to for mothering. They remained close until my mother graduated from high school and left the farm to go to Minneapolis to find work. It was 1943, and World War II was raging. Young men were being drafted, and women were being recruited to work in the war plants on the West Coast. My mother and her best friend, Fern, saw a recruitment poster, bought their train tickets, and returned home to tell their families their plans.

So it was no surprise to Grandma and Grandpa that when Lila graduated from high school, she decided it would be exciting to live with Millie for a while. At the time my mother and I were living in Texas with a man named Gene. In her letters home my mother wrote about hot weather, black-eyed peas, cornbread, and hush puppies. She described people who spoke with accents that came out of their mouths slower than they walked, dabbed their eyebrows with hankies, and drank sweetened tea. Lila was intrigued with the possibility of dating guys she hadn't grown up with in high school, and she thought any job would be better than working on the farm.

On a summer day, Lila kissed her mom and daddy goodbye and boarded a Greyhound bus. What Lila did not know, as the bus passed through Iowa, Missouri, Oklahoma, and Texas, was that she was being delivered into my mother's secrets. Lila was about to replicate her sister's life in ways she could not imagine.

I remember Lila's arrival. My mother was excited to welcome her sister. We had visited the family farm a year earlier in Minnesota when I was four years old. I was very curious about Lila and wondered if I would remember her. It didn't matter. I was so excited to see her that I named my doll Lila.

# 7

## Becoming Prey

### *1951*

Predators look for other people to use, control, or harm in some way. Lila unknowingly landed in the snare of a predator.

Lila arrived in Houston to stay with my mother. She had never traveled away from the family farm, so moving to Texas was a big adventure. Quickly she realized my mother's life with Gene was not what had been described in letters to the family. Gene's violent outbursts and the harsh realities of day-to-day living were grim.

Lila slept on the couch and found a low-paying job. No one knows how she met John, but that day changed the course of her life. He was a thirty-four-year-old man from West Virginia. She was a naïve nineteen-year-old farm girl from Minnesota. They got married, and two months later he found a job in Port Arthur, Texas. He separated her from her sister and kept her away from her family's protection. From his viewpoint, he now owned her in every sense of the word and had a marriage license to prove it.

Years later, in trial testimony, she recounted that they started having difficulty two months after the marriage. John engaged in actions and behaviors common to men who are physically or emotionally abusive. Verbal harassment and belittling comments were the first behaviors and often occurred when John was drinking. Being young and inexperienced, she excused his behaviors and blamed them on the alcohol. It didn't take long before he started checking on her constantly to see where she was. He controlled the money, so she only had the cash he gave her; he kept her name off bank accounts and convinced her that they couldn't afford a bus ticket to visit her sister in Houston. If Lila wrote letters home or to Millie, he read them before they were mailed to see if she was raising any questions about him. He drove her to and from work so he always knew where she was, who she was with, and who her friends were. Everything outside the marriage became a threat.

In time the controlling behavior escalated and became even more dangerous. He yelled, threw things, and slapped her. As many women do, Lila questioned whether she had done something wrong to provoke him. She began watching every word, every move. Before long the physical violence became life-threatening, and Lila was afraid to leave and afraid to stay, held hostage in her own home. She was caught in her predator's snare.

Women in abusive relationships are often asked why they don't leave. To put it simply, Lila was trying to survive. She had been stripped of her humanity and self-worth. Over a period of time, she lost all sense of power and agency in her life. She lost confidence in her ability to take care of herself, and there was the ever-present fear that if she left, he would come after her. She knew he would harm anyone who got in his way. Then the day came when he threatened to slit her throat.

Lila weighed 105 pounds. She was small boned and soft-spoken. John was not a tall man, but he had a thick, muscular build and big hands. His bulging neck supported a square jaw that appeared clenched at all times. He had dark, cold eyes. He could be terrifying if enraged—and he was often enraged.

During her trial testimony, Lila described John's abuse: "He banged my head against the wall and held a knife to my throat." She explained, "He told me if I ever said anything to the law enforcement officer about the beatings, he would cut my head off."

For seven years, Lila endured this treatment. Then John's young unmarried niece had a baby boy and needed someone to care for the baby while she worked. Lila offered to help. The story our family was told was that one day the young woman came home from work and told Lila, "I can't do this anymore. Do you want him?" Lila leaped at the opportunity to become a mother, so she and John prepared to adopt the baby. Now she had to save not only herself but also her son. Motherhood gave Lila a will to live. She determined she had to get closer to home and family if she was going to survive. Somehow Lila persuaded John to move to Minnesota.

They moved to Garrison and rented a trailer on Highway 6 outside town, close to a couple of bars where John found work. During Lila's trial, Greg Mraz, owner of the Y Club, testified about the amount of money John spent on alcohol, which caused audible gasps in the courtroom. He also reported firing John for disorderly conduct. This all occurred within the first six months after John and Lila moved to Minnesota. John's drunkenness and violent behavior escalated more intensely. When he began to threaten the baby, her fear went into overdrive.

## 8

# Thresholds

In 2013, when I first began to research Lila's trial and write Lila's story, I called Tom Fitzpatrick, who had spent his legal career in Brainerd. (Tom is a former law school classmate of my husband.) It was wonderful to talk to an old friend, and when I explained the reason for my contacting him, he said, "You won't believe this coincidence. There's a story in the *Brainerd Daily Dispatch* today about the restoration of two jail cells in the women's wing of the old jailhouse. That's now the Crow Wing County Historical Society." It was the jail where Lila was taken when she was arrested. I needed to see those cells, but my gut tightened at the mere thought. Entering the cells of the past was hard enough, but that jail was the steel and concrete evidence of the pain, chaos, and panic that circled around me when I was thirteen years old.

I remembered an interview in 2011 for *O Magazine* that Maria Shriver conducted with Mary Oliver around the poet's eightieth birthday. Oliver admitted that writing poetry had saved her when she struggled with the sexual abuse she had experienced as a child at the hands of her father. She said, "When you're sexually abused, there's a lot of damage—that's the first time I've ever said that out loud. . . . At this time in my life, I want to be braver."

Reading her words inspired me. I wanted to be brave at this time in my own life and be willing to face the cells of the past, the secrets, mysteries, and unanswered questions, so I drove to Brainerd, checked into a motel, and the next morning arrived at the Crow Wing County Historical Society and Museum.

After I explained the reason for my visit, a staff member showed me around the jailhouse and the family quarters. She showed me the office area where prisoners were brought to be placed under arrest, and then we proceeded upstairs, where the women's cells were located.

I stood in the hallway in silence, looking at the cells. I felt sadness wash over me and turned to the young woman. "May I have a few minutes here by myself?"

"Oh, of course. I'll come back in a bit." I was relieved. I needed to be alone. I stood outside the six-by-eight-foot cell and looked around it, taking in every detail. I thought about what Lila must have felt when she walked into it.

It was so gray: gray metal walls, gray linoleum, gray jail bars. The large door to her cell was gray metal with a tiny opening only large enough to slide a dinner plate through. Along one wall was an iron cot with a gray-and-white mattress. A tiny pillow offered little comfort. On the wall outside the cell were two signs: "Visiting Hours Tues.–Thurs. 2–4 p.m." and "No Visiting at Windows." I realized there probably weren't many visitors to the jail—few people would have been able to visit in the middle of a workday. Opposite the cot was a toilet, stark white in contrast to the gray surroundings and easily visible from the door. In one corner was a small shelf.

I stepped into the jail cell and tried to imagine what it must have been like for my aunt to step across this threshold. My heart pounded. In that instant I felt as if my aunt were inside me. She had been twenty-six years old. Hours before, she had shot and killed her husband. She was placed in this cell by the sheriff and had no idea how long she would be held there. For all she knew in that moment, she might be in a cell like this for the rest of her life. And yet it was perhaps the safest she had felt in seven years of marriage to John. I wondered if she felt relief. I thought about other women who had to take this step to their own freedom and ended up in cells like this.

I knew from Allyn Timmons that her father had told his deputies to be decent to the prisoners because by the time they ended up at the jail, they had already been through a lot. My young aunt had endured years of violence, and by the time she arrived at that jail that night, she had killed her husband with a shotgun, watched his blood pool around his body, and escaped the scene with her baby in her arms. Been through a lot—hell yes!

Allyn also told me about the partnership her mother had with her husband, caring for the prisoners as matron of the jail. I looked at that cell and tried to imagine Mrs. Krueger learning Lila's circumstances from her husband and then visiting Lila that morning. She would have seen bruises around Lila's eyes and her cut lip. Allyn had told me her father said this was one of the worst cases he had ever handled. It probably was for Mrs. Krueger as well. But for Lila, any kindness was a gift. There was nothing more to hide, nothing more to fear. Most importantly, her baby was safe.

I sat down on the bed. I needed to place my hands on this bed, let my eyes rest on the meager details, feel the barren gray and the hardness of the losses that dwelled in that cell that night. I gave thanks that Louise Krueger was there to care for Lila along with her daughters, that there was a good woman present for her. Lila was hungry, and Mrs. Krueger fed her. She was thirsty, and Louise Krueger gave her drink. It was that simple. I appreciated good strong women in my life who had accompanied me through difficult times. Lila had that small grace, so important in the darkness of that hour.

I thanked the kind women in the museum office who had generously extended hospitality to me, a stranger with a story and an odd request to sit in one of their old jail cells. I went to the old courthouse next. It was down the street, easy access for transporting prisoners in the days before the court was moved to a new location in a modern building.

It was a sunny, windy day, a sharp contrast to the gray stillness I had left. The sobering character of the jail cell had moved my thoughts back to the farm the night before the trial.

My mother and I had traveled to the farm that day. Tension was thick in the air. The adults seemed distracted, slightly irritable—talking, but not about what was really on their minds. The gravitational pull of the trial drew relatives and prospective witnesses to the farm, each one trying to find words of reassurance, but mostly showing up to support our family in the only way they knew how.

My uncle Corky arrived by train from California. Bobby, a friend of Lila's who had personally witnessed the results of her beatings, traveled from Texas to testify on her behalf. When my grandfather drove up to the farm after picking Bobby up at the bus station, there was a lot of sobbing as old friends embraced. Beds and cots were borrowed from neighbors to sleep as many as the house could hold. The old wooden wall telephone rang the Palmer farm ring on the rural party line, a long and two shorts, to let everyone know that extended family had arrived in Aitkin, Crosby, or Brainerd. Fresh hay had been put down for the cows; pigs and chickens had been fed. Water had been gathered in cream cans for the baths that would be needed in the morning.

I watched my grandmother and her daughters move back and forth across the kitchen as they multiplied fried salted pork, boiled potatoes, green beans, and pie to feed the crowd of friends and family who had come. I helped set the table. When we gathered around the table for supper, men removed their work caps and women held each other's hands. At age thirteen I was the youngest one at the table, aside from Lila's baby, so I watched the adults for signs of what to expect, what was to come. The usual joking banter and laughter were not there. There was a serious quiet as my grandmother prepared to say the blessing at the last supper before the trial began. It seemed everyone needed to stay strong, be resolute. No one dared let a single crack in the armor be revealed.

I watched Lila. She seemed so young and vulnerable, yet she was held in that circle of family and fed not just meat and potatoes, but strength and faith to carry her through the next several days of the trial, as she had been held and supported during the four months on the farm as she waited. She had spent four days in jail before her bail could be paid, and then she and the baby moved to the farm to live with my grandparents. Normal farm life required a routine, but this time was anything but normal.

The months of waiting for the trial also included the grand jury process. The charge had been changed from first-degree murder to second-degree murder. Meetings were held with lawyers, witnesses were identified, and testimony was prepared. Through it all, everyone in the family cared for Lila's son, the small child in the center of all of this turmoil, sorrow, and trepidation. But on the eve of the trial, all that could be done had been done. Now everyone needed to dwell in faith.

When my grandma bowed her head that evening, every word was a petition, appealing to God to bless so much more than the meal, begging God to protect her daughter, to give the family the strength it would need. "Bless these, thy gifts, which we are about to receive." A simple grace that reached down into our raw selves and comforted our grief and fear. Men who never prayed said out loud, "Amen." At the end of grace, women wiped tears and brushed damp hands on their aprons. It was time to eat and then hope for some sleep.

I remember feeling that in that full farmhouse, at that crowded table, there was no room for my questions or fears. My mother was busy attending to her parents and her sister. I was expected to be strong and soldier on like the rest of the family. I felt lost in the shuffle while others attended to adult business. I was hurt and alone, but I determined that it was my job to understand and to not be a bother. Over the years, I have forgiven my mother and the other adults who were present. They were as lost as I felt. But I learned lessons during that time about not sharing feelings, about putting on a strong veneer despite my edges unraveling, about keeping on a mask of doing okay when everything was not okay. I carried these inhibiting lessons into my adulthood, along with lessons about what it means to stick together as a family, to keep commitments of love, to stand with someone in their worst nightmare. I learned all of that and more than I had words for at the time; however, all those lessons were planted deep.

Lying in bed that night before the trial, I was aware of many people in the house. I heard bedsprings creak as they tossed and turned. Today, I wonder if my grandparents held one another to give each other comfort, to try to anchor themselves so the possible outcomes they imagined wouldn't make them fly away. Or did they lie awake, eyes wide open, each not letting the other know how worried they were, but figuring that if they kept their eyes open, the worst that could happen couldn't sneak up on them during the night? I still remember the squeak of the wooden stairs as family members made their way in the dark to the outhouse to relieve nervous stomachs. The dark night of each soul in that farmhouse inched toward morning, minute by minute.

A gust of wind startled me. I had been lost in my memories, and I suddenly realized I was standing right in front of the courthouse. I had never seen it before. I was not allowed to attend the trial. A friend told me recently that as a little girl, also in the 1950s, she wasn't allowed to attend her own mother's funeral. We easily forget old worldviews about children. My family justified denying my attendance by saying that someone needed to stay home with the baby and my uncle Dale. There was no discussion.

I remember my mother suggesting that it would be too hard for me to hear the details of the night Lila shot John or her life with him. The adults around me seemed to have forgotten my own experiences of violence with my mother at a young age. It did not occur to them that in Lila's story, I might hear a story of power, strength, and courage. At the time, my family was dwelling in the tragedy, shock, and horror of the event, harnessing all their resources to keep Lila out of prison. It left me home on the farm each day, wondering what was happening, feeling left out of this significant event in my family's life. The adults weren't confident that I could handle it even after navigating so much in my own young life.

Each evening, everyone returned from Brainerd exhausted. I gleaned crumbs of information and attempted to piece together what had happened. Listening carefully, I tried to determine if Lila was safe or not safe. This was a threat to the well-being of our entire family. Every day was scary.

For these reasons, I needed to stand in front of the courthouse. I needed to complete the story, the picture, the absence. The stately gray stone facade with black lampposts and Corinthian stone columns gave the building gravitas. I thought about my family arriving here on Monday, November 23, 1959. Most families were preparing for Thanksgiving. My family was preparing for a murder trial.

I entered the courthouse through a large, heavy door and found myself in a foyer that was sleek and elegant, considering the messy affairs of life that had to be settled there. All that stone and the magnified size of doorways and staircases felt very male and powerful. If it made me feel small, I could not imagine how Lila must have felt.

A white marble staircase led upstairs, where the courtrooms were located, I presumed. I walked into the nearest office, shared a bit of my story with a woman who worked there, and asked if I could see the courtroom. Immediately, she grabbed her keys and led me up the marble stairs.

An expansive central atrium with marble columns circled the floor where the courtroom was located. Lining each wall were old, solid-oak benches where my family likely sat for many hours during court recesses. It was difficult to imagine how the members of my common farm family must have felt entering this auspicious space. So much had happened before they ever got to this courthouse that they were steeled for the worst.

Family history can sit in files for years, holding stories, details, and new information. Until the day someone decides it is time to learn more, all of that history sits neglected. I was beginning to recognize refrains of my own mother's story as I investigated Lila's story. I saw parallels between the stories of these two daughters in one family and the incredible strength and courage they both exercised to free themselves, to break the chains that bound them. I was aware of the emotional injuries and devastation I had experienced as a result of these experiences in my own life, and I believed my cousin, Lila's son, was likely carrying the same wounds.

I decided a good place to begin to learn more about this family story was in the newspaper reference files and the case file at the Minnesota History Center. And there it was, beginning with the July 1959 issues of the *Brainerd Daily Dispatch*. It had been there all along, waiting for someone to turn the dial on the microfiche to July 6, 1959. The headline read, "Arraign Garrison Woman in Slaying of Husband: Cries Quiet Tears in Court Here."

The black-and-white photo on the front page of the newspaper shows Lila, accompanied by Sheriff Al Krueger, departing the red-brick jailhouse for municipal court for the arraignment on the charges of murder in the first degree, a charge the grand jury later reduced to second-degree murder. The article goes on to describe Lila as the "admitted shotgun slayer of her 40-year-old bartender husband, John." Camera flashbulbs went off, newspaper reporters crowded around the jailhouse door, and the sheriff escorted her through the crowd.

It took everything within me to not start to sob in that reference library. There it was in black and white. This is what a woman had to do to get herself out of a desperate, violent situation where she felt powerless to change her circumstances. This could have been my own mother.

At the arraignment, Sheriff Krueger and the other officers who had accompanied him to the scene testified that Lila told them "he had been drinking heavily and staying out all night." She went on to testify, "When he got out of the car Saturday morning, I fired both barrels at him. When he got up, I reloaded and shot again. After this, I reloaded again, but he didn't get up." Officers testified that after the shooting, Lila "picked up a two-year-old boy the couple had planned to adopt and went to the neighbors," where she said, "I've shot John."

As I read this account, I thought about my grandparents and mother having to hear this testimony. Did everyone feel regret about not knowing? Did they second-guess themselves about signs or signals they should have seen? Did they suffer for not having done something sooner? They are all gone, so I can't ask them.

I read through the other newspaper articles, which focused on the trial that took place over the Thanksgiving holiday week. It was a strange series of events in our family: a murder on Independence Day and a trial at Thanksgiving. We were a quiet, unassuming family, not inclined to draw attention to ourselves. Here, our family tragedy was smeared all over the front page of the newspapers. In a small town, this wasn't easy. A trip to town to buy groceries, a delivery of milk to the creamery or lumber to a customer could lead to an awkward silence or words of support. The tragedy was on everyone's minds. It was a cross Lila and our family carried for months.

The woman from the office unlocked the courtroom door and allowed me to visit by myself. The courtroom was large, with high ceilings. Large windows lined one whole wall, while large, framed brocade panels filled the other three walls. Most imposing were the judge's large oak bench on one end, an oak jury box along one wall, and rows of long oak benches in the back of the courtroom for those attending the trial. I remembered my uncle Sidney telling me, "People in the area knew there were two good judges in Crow Wing County. Galarneault was one of them."

In my research at the Minnesota History Center, I had learned that John Galarneault Jr. came from a family whose compassion was mythic in the area. His father, John Sr., had owned the Security State Bank during the Great Depression. Unlike other bankers, his father did not close the bank and deny the local farmers, businessmen, and families access to their money. The legend was that his father "took care of the people," according to Sidney, and made sure they had enough to get by. It was expected that this same compassion would carry forth in the life work of John Galarneault's sons.

John Galarneault Jr. had been a judge a little over a year when he was assigned the case *State of Minnesota v. Lila Jean Matheny*. I found myself wondering if this man's compassion was evident in the trial. No transcript exists. Even though I am married to a lawyer and have known many judges in my life, I still felt a sense of awe and wonder over what took place in this courtroom. The warm wood and fine fabric gave it a hospitable feel, but no one would want to be here, especially for a trial involving murder.

I looked at the jury box, and I pondered how it must have felt to those men and women who were questioned about their ability to be impartial in a case like this one. Sidney told me that one of the Twin Cities television stations depicted Lila as an enraged jealous wife who killed her husband over another woman. I wondered whether that influenced the jurors, whose names I found in the case file. The jury included seven men and five women, with one man and one woman as alternates. The women were all identified by their husbands' names. It seemed pretty remarkable that in 1959 there were that many women on the jury, but I suspected this was due to the skillful work of the defense attorney, Joe Ryan.

It is my great regret that I did not begin my research sooner, for Joe Ryan died a few years before I started. One day I called his law firm, and after I explained my mission to the secretary, she gave me the phone number of Jim Ryan, one of Joe's sons. When I called him at home one afternoon and explained the reason for my call, his first response was, "I'll be goddamned! Son of a bitch! I can't believe this. What the hell? Wasn't her husband a bartender at the old Y Club?"

When I said yes, he went on, "Hell yes, I remember. Wasn't her name Lila Matheny? That was a hell of a case. I was in my teens, maybe around eighteen at the time. My father had to go to the scene of the shooting, so I tagged along. I still remember seeing the brown bloodstains on the ground. Wasn't there a fundraising dance for your family to help pay the legal bills?" When I said yes, he reminded me that his father had taken him and all of his brothers to the dance.

I wanted to know more about the man his father was. "Well, he was a tough, no-nonsense father. He did a lot of different kinds of cases as a small-town lawyer. My dad was a hell of a man. I can't tell you the number of people that would stop me in town and tell me that if they could have gone to a cheaper lawyer they would have, but if a person was in real trouble, they would go to my dad."

Joe Ryan, as it turned out, had known his own losses and understood tragedy and its impact on a family. When his daughter was a toddler, she wandered down to the Mud River behind the family home and drowned. It was a devastating blow to Joe and his wife, Carol. In addition, one of his sons, Jack, suffered a cerebral hemorrhage in a high school football accident that left him unable to live independently for the rest of his life. Joe Ryan understood trauma and grief. It meant something to me to speak to someone close to the man who had stood by my aunt Lila in the worst of circumstances.

As I looked at the rows of seats where the people who attended the trial sat, I remembered reading in one article, "Veteran courtroom observers said it was the first murder in the area since 1940, when a youth was charged with shooting his father." The reporter noted the size of the crowd: "Latecomers were forced to stand along the sides and rear wall of the chamber." He also noted the presence of women in the courtroom, who "arrived early and in large numbers."

He wrote, "The high point of the early morning testimony came when the attractively dressed defendant told sobbingly and haltingly how she was beaten more than six years ago and threatened with her life if she revealed the beating." He reported that she said, "He banged my head against the wall and held a knife to my throat." The reporter commented that "sympathetic looks among the women spectators were exchanged as Mrs. Matheny testified of the brutal treatment she received at the hands of her dead husband."

Joe Ryan likely traced this pattern over many years for the benefit of the jury. There was no denying the violence that had led to Lila's actions. I sat in the courtroom on that gray morning, grateful for those women showing up, whoever they were and whatever reason brought them there each day.

I noted the two tables where the lawyers sat, one table for the defendant and her lawyer and the other for the prosecuting attorney, Carl Erickson. My uncle Sidney told me that Carl Erickson was a "shyster" and not highly regarded in the county. According to the newspaper articles on the trial, Erickson used drama to generate some excitement in the courtroom when he put what appeared to be loaded shells into the double-barreled shotgun used in the slaying. The reporter wrote, "At the click of the closing, spectators drew in their breath in a mass inhalation audible throughout the courtroom." Judge Galarneault "immediately halted the proceedings as he addressed Mr. Erickson. 'I'd appreciate it if you'd unload that gun in my court, Mr. Erickson.'"

I sat in that courtroom and felt the dread my family must have felt the day the jury went into deliberations. The newspaper headline had read, "Jury Expected To Receive Lila Matheny Case Today." The possible outcomes were devastating. In a small town, how this story was interpreted in the news was important. I believe those women showing up in the courtroom each day, as well as the women on the jury, made all the difference. Joe Ryan asked the jury to "judge Mrs. Matheny's conduct on the basis of seven years of brutal treatment she received at the hands of her husband." Then he rested his case.

I also believe Joe Ryan was instrumental in the outcome of this trial. I found requests he had written to be included in the judge's instructions to the jury. His instructions included these points:

- That the defendant is presumed innocent, that her indictment by a grand jury and her presence in court charged with a crime prove nothing and should not be considered by the jury as evidence of guilt.
- That it is not disputed that the defendant took the life of her husband, but that the defendant claims that her act was justified and that this homicide was justifiable under the law of this state (MSA 619.29).
- That the burden of proof does not rest upon the defendant to prove that this homicide was justifiable. The burden of proof is entirely

upon the State to satisfy and convince you beyond a reasonable doubt that the defendant's act was not justifiable. If you do have a reasonable doubt, then it is your duty to bring in a verdict of not guilty.

- That if it appeared that the defendant had reasonable grounds to apprehend a design on the part of John Matheny to do some great personal injury to her, and if it appeared to her that there was imminent danger of his carrying out that design, then her act in taking his life was justifiable.

- That it was not necessary for the defendant to wait to be physically attacked and harmed by Matheny to be justified in her act. She had a legal right to forestall and prevent such harm when it appeared to her that she had ground to expect great and imminent harm to her from John Matheny.

- That evidence was introduced regarding the character, reputation, and personal traits of the defendant in order to assist you in determining whether the defendant had any criminal intent. It was also for the purpose of aiding you in determining whether the defendant acted out of fear for her own safety under the definition of justifiable homicide that I have given you.

Once the judge issued his instructions to the jury, they began their deliberation at 4:45 p.m. Lila's life was in the hands of that jury.

I am in awe of Lila's strength on the witness stand. She had to tell her story, every detail, before a crowd of strangers, never knowing whether they believed her or not. Exposing all the shameful and humiliating treatment she suffered while telling her truth took courage. I sat in that courtroom and felt proud of my aunt and my family. At the most threatened time in our family's memory, they held their heads high, persevered, and did their utmost to save Lila. They had scrounged up thousands of dollars for her defense and supported and cared for her through grueling legal meetings and trial preparation. They did everything they could.

I remembered a story Sidney had told me.

Every day of the trial, my family and a few close friends went for lunch at a little Greek restaurant close to the courthouse. They often had the place to themselves. The owners, a Greek gentleman and his wife and family, fed and cared for my family. Each day during the trial, that family read the newspaper over breakfast, followed Lila's story, and waited for the Palmers to appear at lunch.

On the day the jury began its deliberation, my family returned to the restaurant for dinner. The owners already knew the dishes my family liked, so they brought out platters of food, serving family style. My family members hardly noticed, they were so preoccupied. They simply ate.

This meal provided a respite, a breaking of bread and communion until they had to return to the courthouse and reality. At the end of the meal, my grandfather and Sidney went to the cash register to pay the bill. The Greek gentleman looked my grandfather right in the eye and said gently, "No, Mr. Palmer. Your family has been through enough. Let us do this small kindness for you." He would not allow my grandfather to pay and insisted that my family members were their guests that evening. In this instance, the stranger provided the welcome. Fifty-five years later, Uncle Sidney cried telling me this story. Compassion and kindness are never forgotten.

I left that courtroom feeling I had visited sacred ground. Hell had been experienced in that place, and the door to grace was opened, both at a Greek restaurant and in a verdict. I looked back at those oak benches once again, imagining the hours my family sat there waiting for the jury to return with its verdict. The jury had returned two times with additional questions for the judge, each time heightening my family's tension and anxiety. Then, at last, the jurors returned at 1:30 a.m. The judge asked, "Will the jury foreman please stand? Has the jury reached a unanimous verdict?"

"We have, your honor."

The clerk took the paper from the foreman and handed it to the judge to be read silently. The judge handed the paper back to the clerk to be read aloud. "The defendant is not guilty."

My aunt and uncle told me that the jury members hugged Lila as they left the courtroom. Sidney commented, "I just remember the relief of it."

When he heard about the verdict, John Matheny's brother threatened to come to Minnesota and kill our entire family. The men in my family slept with loaded guns by their beds for weeks after the trial.

This place was a part of my family history. What happened here altered my family forever.

# 9

## From My View

In my teenage world, I just wanted to be normal. I didn't want to stick out or draw attention to myself. As an only child being raised by a single mother, I learned I was already an oddity in the Ozzie, Harriet, David, and Ricky days. The 1950s TV show *The Adventures of Ozzie and Harriet* painted the picture of the ideal American family, only surpassed by *Father Knows Best*, with the father at the helm away at work all day while the mother worked in the home, wearing an apron and the perfect hairdo. I never talked about my home life at school. I wouldn't dream of telling about the miles my mother and I had traveled already in my young life or the traumas we had experienced.

And then—*bang bang!* Two shots rang out on a hot summer night. I wasn't there, but I might as well have been. Those shots passed right through me and tore into bones of anxiety, wrenching loose tissues of terror I had buried down deep. Those shots broke open memories and shook the security I was seeking as a young woman and beginning to establish in my small world. *Bang bang!* I fell. I watched my mother fall, members of my family fall. We all lay on the ground of our being, in shock, horror, fear, each of us experiencing new wounds to old injuries, but no one talked about them. The serenity of our life on the farm was shattered. I didn't know what would happen to us—to me.

My mother, grandparents, this family was all I had. If they fell, what would happen to me? If they didn't make it, I wouldn't make it. They were my life, my foundation, but the foundation had been shaken. I didn't feel safe. Alert for danger, I watched. I listened.

That summer when Lila shot her husband, I was moving into adolescence and my first awareness of boy-girl relationships. I was beginning to experience crushes and an attraction to boys. This was confusing because I already had a deep distrust and fear of men. Lila's experience took me back to an earlier time in my childhood of not feeling safe. That is what drove Lila to pull the trigger: not feeling safe. The last time I had felt that scared was when I was six years old and my mother and I lived with Gene in Texas. As hard as I had worked to feel strong within myself, I was that little girl again. John Matheny was a scary man. I had seen this scary man before, but then I was little and powerless. I didn't have a gun.

I wanted to talk to my mother about those past scary times, but I didn't. I wanted to seek reassurance, but I didn't. My mother was a master of burying secrets and sending the signal "Off Limits." It may have been her own shame and humiliation over these experiences, but because she didn't talk openly with me, they became my shame and humiliation as well. Not talking left open-ended questions that remained unresolved and unhealed.

The adults around me couldn't talk about anything other than the facts: chores to be done, meetings with lawyers, money for legal fees. What mattered was getting up, getting busy. I now know this is what people do when they are grieving, but I did not know that then.

My family had been vulnerable before—to winds, frost, storms, downed trees, washed-out roads, and drought. They had dealt with a cow having a breech birth or a pig having stillborn babies. They knew what it meant to have matters out of your control, but somewhere in all of that uncertainty, they prayed that some greater goodness would be merciful.

I had lived with my grandparents on the farm every summer while my mother worked in Minneapolis. I had observed their tenacity. I witnessed their faith in one another, hard work, and something greater than themselves. I believe my grandfather pondered these things when the ground was as hard as concrete and could break a plow or when a hayfield didn't produce. I believe my grandmother prayed over these things when there were not enough vegetables in the garden to can and put aside in her root cellar or when a cow went dry and there was less milk and less cream to churn into butter. My grandparents were able to touch and feel the forces that hauled them to the brink, but this time was about being out on the edge of a catastrophe they had not experienced before.

After the shooting, even I could see that this was a different kind of out-of-control that hit my family. My family had to rely on others who had knowledge in legal matters and the law. This system was not a system of natural laws, God giving or God taking away. This male-directed system involved cunning, strategy, gavels, black robes, power, authority, and jail bars. This was a system with men at the center, men in charge, and men making the decisions.

During that summer, I picked up my milk pails and headed to the barn. I comforted myself by placing my head against the warm body of each cow as I milked. I appreciated the scent of the warm milk and fresh hay, listened as the cows chewed their cud, and appreciated the quiet. I also took care of the baby that summer while Lila and the family attended meetings with lawyers and prepared for the trial. I fed him, bathed him, and played with him, knowing he was in his own tender time. I comforted him the way I wanted to be comforted. I held him the way I wanted to be held.

In the midst of the turmoil and absence of being attended to myself, I learned some important positive lessons that summer. I watched Lila. I learned what it means to be a strong woman, to do what needs to be done to save yourself and your child, if necessary. As Lila's story slowly opened up, I learned what she had to endure and I saw how her experience echoed my own mother's experience. I witnessed how the love of a family can carry someone through the worst experience of their life. I watched my mother be strong for everyone in the family.

I also saw my mother's worry, her hands shaking, her more frequent smoking. I heard her moving around at night, unable to sleep. My mother had been ill off and on in my elementary school years with pneumonia and lung problems. One hospitalization lasted a month; my aunt Della came to stay with me. My mother gave me four envelopes, each holding a five-dollar bill, so I would have spending money. The whole experience was very unsettling. My biggest fear was that I would lose my mother, and it remained my biggest fear to the day she died. Years later, Della and Sidney told me, "She bore the brunt of everything."

What I overheard in family conversations confirmed what I already knew about violent men: they want to rule and will hurt anyone who gets in their way. I determined very early in life I was never going to tolerate any dominant behavior from any man. As I watched my grandfather, I also learned that some men can be steadfast, gentle, and strong. I held onto that model as well.

I returned to Minneapolis at the end of the summer to attend junior high school. I didn't tell my friends or teachers what had happened over the summer. I hid the story and my feelings. I was ashamed, embarrassed, and I felt an otherness that dealt with something too dark. It was an abyss I could not cross with my friends—violence and murder. The media coverage mentioned family names that were not mine, so no one was the wiser. I grew a mask that I lived behind. I began my first venture into dual selves as I attended boy-girl parties, played tennis at the park with friends, and went to slumber parties, pretending to be happy, acting as if nothing was wrong. I got really good at wearing a mask and carried this skill well into adulthood.

My mother had always worked two or three jobs, but now she added on supporting Lila and my grandparents as well. I knew she was frightened that Lila could go to prison for life and about the impact this would have on my grandparents. I watched my mother's suffering, worry, and courage as she supported all those around her.

Through it all, my mother and I never discussed how this trauma made the dry bones of our own past rise up from the grave to haunt each of us again. Today, I have a deeper understanding that we were, in fact, protecting and caring for each other. Silence became a habit as the memories of our own terrifying escape from violence, though different from Lila's, came rushing into the present. It was a past that would need healing in its own time, so we did what we had always done for each other. We persevered.

# Part 3

# Millie's Choice

A girl was like a kite; without her mother's strong, steady hold on the string, she might just float away, be lost somewhere among the clouds.

—Kristin Hannah, *The Great Alone*

## 10

# Birth of Secrets

## *1946*

I was conceived in Portland, Oregon, gestated in Seattle, Washington, and born in Costa Mesa, California, on February 12, 1946. I had put on many miles before I took my first breath. My conception was a chrysalis of secrets that began to be spun in April 1944.

Two Minnesota farm girls, my mother, Millie, and her best friend, Fern, responded to a posting by the Army Air Corps in the *Minneapolis Tribune*, recruiting workers for the Boeing aircraft plants in Seattle to support the war effort. The two of them took the trolley car to the state employment service, filled out applications, and then walked out with two train tickets in their hands. Then they went home to tell their parents what they had done. They were about to set off on a big adventure.

Traveling west on the train, they saw the Rocky Mountains and young soldiers in uniform for the first time. Who knows which was more dazzling? They met a couple of soldiers who helped them get into the dining car reserved only for military service personnel. When they arrived in Seattle, they saw the camouflage-painted roof of Boeing Plant Number 2. The serious nature of war and the threat of attack were sobering to their naïve, adventurous spirits.

A contact person met them at the train station, drove them to Renton, thirteen miles from Seattle, and oriented them to Plant Number 9. There they joined the eighteen million women who worked during the war, three million of them in war plants—young women who had responded to the same patriotic appeal.

Millie and Fern were housed in Cedar River Park, an apartment complex built to accommodate the influx of laborers from all over the country. Even though my mother missed her parents, brothers, and sisters, these were war years, and many families were being wrenched apart.

When Millie and Fern showed up for work the first day there were few men in the plant, but they were the ones in charge. They were the managers and union leaders. Many of these men were too old to be drafted, so they were protective of their entitled roles and did not seem to like managing women. If my mother and Fern had hoped to do anything other than line work, it wasn't going to happen. All around them were capable women with skills as good as or better than those of their male counterparts, but women were not given a chance at better, higher-paying job opportunities.

Fern shared many of these details when she wrote to me decades later, when she was in her nineties. She described the Seattle area during the war as teeming with servicemen. "It was an exciting time and place to be living. We were all young and probably thought we had the world by the tail." When my mother and Fern, along with their friends Wilma and Fran, were not working, they were at the officers' and servicemen's dances, parties, pavilions, and parks where soldiers gathered to meet single women. Romances began; declarations of love and commitment were made; rings and ID bracelets were exchanged. Popular singer Dinah Shore sang "Something to Remember You By," and then young men went off to war. Sometimes the women were left with more to remember them by than they had bargained for.

A picture in my mother's photo album shows my mother, Fern, Fran, and Wilma walking down the street in Seattle, arm in arm, dark-haired, young, beautiful, confident. They all wore stylish pleated slacks and overcoats with shoulder pads. They were in a new city with new jobs, making new friends. Aside from the war, they didn't have a care in the world, though they were learning quickly the lessons and losses of conflict, hard work, survival, and interrupted love stories. Then, in 1945, my mother moved to Portland, Oregon, to work in a new plant.

# 11

# Motherhood

I don't have memories of my mother telling me stories of my birth, her eyes dewy as she remembered the essential experience that made her a mother. I don't have memories of my mother telling me how she got pregnant, what it was like to carry me in her belly, recalling the first contraction, her labor, her joy at seeing my face for the first time, or feeling glad I was a little girl. She never said anything about holding me in her arms, swaddling me for the first time, whether she nursed me or not.

I suspect she never told me because these memories were painful because she was alone. I have joked over the years about my beginnings, but I know I have used humor to cover my loss, for there is a deep sadness in this story. I only know what I know from Fern, who joined my mother in Los Angeles a few months after I was born.

I called Fern the day after my mother died unexpectedly on New Year's Eve in 1975. Her death was a shock. My mother's life had never been more hopeful. Her health had been good. She had started college that fall to get a degree in chemical dependency counseling and was excited about her work helping chemically dependent individuals transition into the workplace following treatment. Fern had only heard wonderful news in recent letters from my mother, so she was stunned and devastated to hear of my mother's death.

After I explained the circumstances, we talked for a while. Then Fern asked me, "Did your mother ever tell you anything about your father?"

"No, she didn't. I always wondered why he never wanted to find me or know who I am."

"Well, I knew him," she said quietly.

"What? You did? All these years and you never said anything." There it was. A matter-of-fact secret kept from me for twenty-nine years. A sense of betrayal was beginning to creep into my gut.

"Well, I always thought if your mother wanted you to know, she would've told you."

"Well, I don't care who he is—if he is in prison or a mental hospital somewhere—I want to know who he is. If you know anything about him, I have a right to know." I was feeling indignant that she might withhold information from me.

"Let me think about it and call you back."

"Are you kidding me? My mother is dead. Why would she care? Why would you care?" Now I was raising my voice, close to shouting at her on the telephone.

"Let me think about it. I'll call you back. I promise. I need some time to think. I'm so sorry about your mother. I've lost a dear friend."

I could tell she was crying as she hung up. I sat there looking at the telephone receiver in my hand, adrenaline pumping through my system. It took every ounce of energy I had to not call her right back and rage at her.

A couple weeks later the phone rang. It was Fern. "Karla, I've been thinking about you so much since we last talked."

"Well, that's nice, but I don't understand why you couldn't just tell me what you know."

"I know it's hard to understand. Your mother was a dear friend, and we went through a lot together. I was worried about your mother and what she would think. I want you to know I consulted with a Catholic priest friend of mine. He said that if I had information that I knew about your life at all, you deserved to know."

"Well, thank goodness, someone is being reasonable." I wasn't feeling very forgiving.

"He said I owed it to you to tell you. He said your mother is dead, and we owe the truth to the living. I want to tell you the whole story, but I want to be with you when I do. I'll come out to Minneapolis this spring, and then we'll talk."

"Well, thank you. I'm glad you're willing to tell me what you know. I'll be anxious for your visit." I cared for Fern and didn't want to make it any more difficult for her. I had to be content with waiting, but at least I knew the information would be forthcoming.

That spring, Fern and I met at Annie's Parlour at Lake and Hennepin, a burger joint with loud rock-and-roll music playing in the background. It was an inauspicious place for an important conversation, but it was an upbeat place, which was what we needed.

Fern said, "I'm not sure where to begin, but I think it's important to understand what the war years were like. There were a lot of young people on the West Coast. It was an intense time. Men and women were meeting. Everything felt urgent, rushed. Men were being shipped out. Couples never knew how much time they had together."

I listened, hungry for every detail.

"Your mother and I were in Portland, Oregon, for a short time, working in one of the war plants there. That's where your mother met your father. We actually double-dated." She continued slowly, "Your mother was a good woman. She didn't play around with a lot of men. But when she met your father, it was serious for her."

I waited anxiously to learn his identity.

"Your father was a soldier and worked in the military hospital in Vancouver, Washington." She looked me directly in the eyes, searching my face to see how I was taking this. And then she told me, "Your father's name is Joseph Hyder."

There. That was his name. It took my breath away to hear it because it wasn't the name on my birth certificate. I had never thought of myself as part German. Irish, English, Scotch, and a little Swedish, maybe, but not German.

"He was a very good-looking guy. If you think you look like your mother, you really look like your father." This information set me back in my seat. It brought this stranger closer somehow. "He was very athletic and an outdoorsman. You may get that from him. He was educated and came from a very good family. It's funny what a person remembers, but I remember he drove a beautiful convertible."

Suddenly I felt something come over me. I was someone I didn't know I was. It was a strange awareness—German! A man I didn't know, but I looked like him.

"Your mother fell deeply in love with Joe. Soon they were engaged. It didn't take long, though, before she discovered he was cheating on her. She wasn't going to tolerate that, so she left Portland and went back to Seattle to live with me. She went back to work at the Boeing plant in Renton. But soon after, she discovered she was pregnant. She was so hurt, she chose not to tell Joe."

My mother was twenty years old, single, and pregnant. My father never knew I was born; he never knew he had a daughter walking around in the world. I had spent my life wondering why he never tried to find me. I thought he didn't care. Now I understood: he never knew I existed.

In 1945 a pregnant single woman carried an enormous stigma. A child born outside marriage was considered illegitimate, and the child carried that label for the rest of their life. According to Fern, there were many young women in my mother's situation. They had fallen in love with servicemen who had left for the war, and then they discovered they were pregnant. Some young men were sympathetic and willing to help a woman friend with a speedy marriage. If the two felt affection, it was a bonus.

My mother met one of those young men: Charles. He had been interested in her when she first arrived in Seattle. When she left Joe and moved back, Charles connected with her right away. He asked her to marry him. There wasn't much time before I was to be born. Fern wanted me to understand my mother's choice. "I think your mother felt this was the only way out of a tough situation. I think she really hoped she could make it work. Charles was a nice, thoughtful, gentle man, so she said yes, and they got married. He was the only man who truly loved your mother."

There wasn't much to learn about my mother's wedding. Fern said it took place in front of a justice of the peace. It made me sad to imagine that day for my mother, a day that is supposed to be one of the most joyful in a woman's life. I wondered if she thought of Joe that day and how different her life and mine might have been if he had been a man who kept his commitments.

Fern went on to tell me that within weeks after the wedding, my mother knew it wouldn't work. Not only did she have an illegitimate pregnancy, she now also had an illegitimate marriage, one without love. As kind and compassionate as Charles was to her, she didn't love him, so she left.

Leaving was a pattern for my mother even at that young age. I can see that she had limits to what she could tolerate. She was brave and willing to go it alone if that was what it took to have her integrity. I realized that, without even knowing it, I had become my mother over the years.

"Your mother's sister Bernie and her husband lived in Southern California at the time. She moved in with them." Pregnant, no job, two failed relationships, and miles away from home—a tough spot for a young woman. When she entered Labor and Delivery at Orange County Hospital, anything could have happened. Many young women in similar situations were relinquishing their babies. I can't conceive of the courage it took for my mother to walk out of that hospital with a baby in her arms. She knew the stigma was great and the financial resources were scarce.

Fern looked at me across the table. She said, "If your mother had a flaw, it was that she loved too hard."

"What does that mean?"

"Well, she planted her heart in the wrong men. She went for the good-looking guys, but they weren't always the nicest guys."

What I do know is that my mother left the hospital after my birth committed to making a life for the two of us. In 1946 this might have been a brave decision or a foolish one, but for certain it wasn't going to be easy.

My mother was twenty-one years old, had a child, and needed to find work. It put her on the move, searching for a job, any job, and a place to live. After my mother died, I found a list of all the places she had lived in my early years: it revealed three months here, four months there. I was left with strangers who cared for me while she worked, people she had to trust. She had no choice.

What I do know is she loved me with every ounce of her being. She loved me by remaining steadfast through poor decisions, poor health, and poverty. I remember, as a child, my mother sitting by my bed after she thought I was asleep. She would just sit and look at me. Sometimes, I thought I heard her crying. I believe there were times when I was all that kept her going forward. She couldn't give up. As I grew up, we became a team, mother and daughter, alone together in the days of the perfect *Leave It to Beaver* family. We were two women, independent, brave. I learned at a young age that men weren't necessary and, in fact, could make life feel less safe.

When I cleaned out my mother's apartment after she died, I found her journal. In it she had recorded a Blessings List. Number one on her list: "Thank you for my wonderful daughter." And also, "Thank you for my wonderful parents, my wonderful sisters and brothers, for being able to work, a comfortable apartment, spiritual support, kindness of others, for making Schatzie, Karla's dog, well, for my daughter's success, happiness, and blessings." Even though her life had been hard, she lived in a state of deep gratitude.

My mother's love for me reminds me of a line from Barbara Kingsolver's book *The Bean Trees*: "There were two things about Mama. One is she always expected the best out of me. And the other is that no matter what I did, whatever I came home with, she acted like it was the moon I had just hung up in the sky and plugged in all the stars. Like I was that good." Despite her remarkable love for me, the mystery surrounding my birth and the secret of my father left me with an ambivalence about where men fit into our lives. I yearned for male affection and affirmation. Even with all that love, I still had a lifetime of questions and a hole inside myself that couldn't seem to be filled.

# 12

## Gene

❧ ❧

There is no greater agony than bearing an untold story inside you.

—Maya Angelou

How and where my mother met Gene, I am not sure. It could have been in California, Arizona, or Nevada, as we moved constantly. Consistency, routine, security: these were not my experience as a baby or young child.

I have my own memories of Gene—memories laid down inside me when I was too young to have words for what I experienced, for what I saw. Gene was a tall man with dark curly hair and ice-blue eyes that danced over his beguiling smile. Looking at him in photos in my mother's old photo album, I can see how she might have been attracted to him. There are photos of us looking like a happy threesome. My mother had taken Gene's last name so her family and friends would believe they were married. Going through my mother's papers after her death, I learned they were never married, another secret my mother kept. But unmarried couples were not supposed to cohabitate in the 1950s, so this was easier.

"Do you ever have any memories of when you were young?" Fern asked me.

Sitting in Annie's Parlour, I looked across the table as she took a drink of coffee and a deep breath as if to fortify herself. I realized there was more to come in this conversation.

"I have memories. I remember Gene." Memories flooded over me in an instant—darkness, forced touching, Gene hurting my mother, being frightened when he came into a room. I could feel anxiety creeping up the core of my body, but I didn't talk about any of it because I never had. I wanted to hear what she had to say.

"Well, there's something you need to know. It may help you. There were things that happened to you before you could even talk, before you had language. It may help you to understand yourself and your mother a bit better." She paused. "If you ever feel anxiety, fear, unexplainable terror that blindsides you for what seems to be no reason, there is a reason. You need to know where these feelings are coming from. You need to know you experienced violence even before you had words as a child. You saw a lot. You experienced a lot."

Fern kept talking, choosing her words with care. It was as if she felt a responsibility in my mother's absence to tell me what she felt I needed to know. Looking back on that moment, I felt a tender loving kindness from my mother's dearest, lifelong friend. Despite some early challenges in her own life, Fern had moved forward, married, and had a beautiful family, including three children. She was a very intelligent woman who had grown personally and had created a marriage and life my own mother was never able to achieve. Over all the years, Fern loved my mother and, in turn, loved me. In this moment, that love was revealed in truth-telling to deepen my own self-awareness and understanding.

"Your mother met Gene when you were very little. She was single, alone, trying to do it by herself, trying to take good care of you. She was always on the move, one lousy waitress and hostess job after another. She found bosses and landlords could be troublesome to an attractive single woman. They wanted more than work or rent, so she moved on. I think she just got tired."

She took another swallow of coffee. "So she took up with Gene. He seemed to be a nice enough guy, but not long after they were together, his true side came out. He was pretty rough with her at times. Your mother seemed to think that if she loved him hard enough, he would quit hurting her." Fern took another deep breath, as if dreading what she was about to say, but her eyes held a steel resolve.

"There was one night that Gene was beating your mother. She was terrified he would hurt you. When he was in the bathroom, she grabbed you and ran two blocks to the apartment building where Joe and I lived. She was afraid to involve me, but she didn't know where else to go. All I had to do was look at her to know this time was different. We managed our apartment building, so we hid you and your mother in an empty apartment. Gene came to the door and pounded on it with his fist. He yelled your mother's name. We were terrified to open the door, but we knew we had to. When we did, he stood there holding a butcher knife. Joe told him he had better leave or we would call the police. Your mother stayed in that dark empty apartment and held you in her arms through the night. We were all afraid Gene might return. That was just one of many times."

"How soon did she go back to him?' I didn't really want to hear the answer.

"The next day. She couldn't stay in hiding. There were no shelters in those days. Of course, he promised it would never happen again. I think she loved him. She wanted to believe him. Times were hard. It was tough for a woman to make it on her own with a child. And she had done it for so long." Fern sighed, as if she was relieved she no longer had to bear this story alone.

I sat there feeling sad, grateful to her, and overwhelmed. For years I had tried to decode feelings, emotions, reactions, and responses I had that did not seem appropriate to the moment I was in. Now I understood why. I was just beginning to recall buried memories, and Fern's words filled in the blank spaces in my past.

When I was around three years old, Gene, my mother, and I moved to Houston. We lived in a house on a street with lots of trees. I remember my aunt Lila came to Texas to be with us, but she wasn't with us long. She met a man, got married, and moved away.

I remember the house we lived in. The living room was where my mother and I spent happy times together. A floor-model radio stood in a corner. It had big black knobs that turned on and off, raised the volume, and lit up a little screen with numbers on it. My mother and I would sit in front of the radio in the evening listening to stories. She would stitch her embroidery, and I would color in my coloring book or play with my doll, Lila. We faced the radio, as if we believed we could see the characters inside the stories. We listened to mysteries like *The Shadow, The Creaking*

*Door*, and *Mr. and Mrs. North*. We laughed out loud to *Fibber McGee and Molly* or sang along with Dinah Shore.

I remember the bedroom in that house, but mostly I remember the bed. That was where Gene held my mother down to hurt her until she cried. I could only watch while I huddled in the corner. My mother had a waitress job at night, so when Gene came home from work, she would leave me with him. I remember the darkness of that bedroom. I remember being on that bed with sheets, piles of sheets, being lost in sheets. Gene told me what to do. He made me touch hard objects. As a small child, I didn't know the hard object was his body. It was dark. I did what I was told. I put my hands where I was told. I put my mouth where I was told. I remember grunting sounds and being touched.

My mother was never there beside me to help me or hold me. I remember Gene telling me, "You keep your mouth shut about this, you hear. If you don't, I will really hurt your mother." I never slept on that bed. I moved to sleep on the couch in the living room when Gene fell asleep. I never told my mother about the sheets.

The bathroom in that house was all white with shiny tiles. There were times when Gene was angry and my mother got nervous. In a hurry, she would fill the bathtub and place me in the tub to stay and play by myself. I was left to entertain myself for long periods of time. I discovered that I could roll toilet paper into the tub and make wads of wet paper. With a good toss, I could get the wads of paper to stick to the bathroom ceiling, where they dried and puffed up like snowballs. Sometimes, I could hear scary banging noises outside the bathroom, so I sang to block out the sounds. I had heard Patti Page sing "I Went to Your Wedding" on the radio, a song about an old lover attending the wedding of his beloved who was marrying another man. Everyone was crying, most due to happiness, but this man was singing with sorrow. As I sang the words, I would add my own sobs and tears, gradually becoming dramatic and loud. Sometimes I could work my way to my own real tears—tears of fear, bewilderment, and sorrow.

In my forties, when I went to seminary, I began deep therapy. With the help of Dick Jones, a skilled therapist, I began to rustle around in the dark corners of my history. The more cobwebs I cleared, the more anxious I became. I locked doors, heard strange sounds at night, and was reluctant to be home alone. My children were young, and I regretted my anxiety. I wanted to be a strong mother. I wanted my children to feel secure. I felt as if I wasn't tethered to the ground, undone by the simplest thing, and there seemed to be nothing I could do about it. Until, one day, Dick said, "I want you to go home and tell your husband what you're going through and how scared you are. To really show him, I want you to ask him to buy you a baseball bat. Then keep that bat beside your bed so you feel safe." It was a very difficult thing to do, to concede that I was so frightened. I didn't ask for help easily, believing I had to do everything by myself.

Even though he was a bit bewildered, my husband, Willie, knew I was going through a difficult time. Without any questions, he bought me the baseball bat. It was one of the most loving things he could ever do for me.

For months during this time I was awakened in the early morning hours by the sound of an organ playing. The music was loud and always the same: it sounded like the serious organ music of British organist E. Power Biggs. I wondered which of my neighbors was playing the organ at such odd hours. One morning I quietly slipped out of bed, tiptoed past my sleeping children's rooms, went downstairs, and opened the sliding glass door to the deck. I stuck my head out into the darkness, saw the old oak tree standing vigil, and heard nothing. Yet the organ music went on for months. In time, with Dick's help, I came to understand that the organ music was inside me, buried in sheets of memory.

After two years, therapy had run its course. I was stuck, frozen in grief. I could not get down to the bedrock of emotions to feel rage about what I had experienced as a child. Dick suggested I try hypnosis. I was skeptical, but I was willing to try anything. I felt as if I had been crying for two years, mourning what had happened to me.

Cautiously, and with some skepticism, I went to the office of a very kind woman whose work Dick respected. It took several tries, but in one session, under hypnosis, I had a vision of the kitchen in the house in Houston. I stood there as an adult woman and saw myself as a little girl sitting in a kitchen chair at the table with Gene, who had his back to me. Gene was screaming at the little girl, pounding his fist on the table, thrashing his arms around. I saw the terrified look on the little girl's face.

I couldn't stand it any longer. I needed to help her, so I approached him from behind, grabbed him around the throat, and strangled him with my bare hands.

The rage that I released as I squeezed his neck surged through my hands, providing strength I didn't know I had. I squeezed until my arms hurt. I wanted to know he was dead, finished, gone. He was. As soon as I was out of the session, I called Dick and said, "I murdered him with my bare hands."

After that day, I put the baseball bat away. The organ music stopped.

## 13

## Escape

### *1952*

The most dangerous time for a woman in a violent relationship is when she attempts to leave. Attempting to leave with children is even more dangerous and complicated. My mother went into hiding with me some time before we escaped Houston. There is a long period that is completely blank for me. I have no memory of where we were, who was there, or if someone helped us. I believe this time is blank because my terror was that great. Gene wasn't there, but I knew we were hiding from him.

My mother and I had a "lean on each other" relationship. As an only child and an only parent, we formed our own galaxy, our souls orbiting each other, mother-daughter gravity keeping us on course even when other forces pulled on us with a vengeance. I never doubted she loved me fiercely.

When I was a child, at night after I had been tucked in for a while, my mother would sometimes come and sit next to the couch where I slept and smoke a cigarette. I could smell the smoke, hear her breathing. I would lie still so she wouldn't know that I knew she was there. She would stroke my forehead and then lean over and kiss my forehead, saying softly, "I love you, Sugarfoot." Kids know when adults are scared. Living with Gene, we had a lot to be scared about every single day. I watched my mother closely, gauging our well-being at any moment. I saw her hands shake, watched her bite her lips, saw her reach for a cigarette over and over when things got tense. Like a contagious disease, her fear spread to me. God only knows how many years we were both infected before my mother took the risk to save us both. Then something happened. True grit and determination replaced her fear.

I remember my mother getting me out of bed late one night to go to the bus depot. "You have to get up, sweetheart. I know you haven't slept very long, but we're going on a trip. We're going to see Grandma and Grandpa. I have your clothes laid out, so just get up and get dressed." We had visited my grandparents once, so visiting them on their farm made me happy. I remember my mother peering out the window, watching for our ride. I remember riding in a strange woman's car to the bus depot.

The depot was really big; there were people sitting on benches everywhere. I watched my mother buy tickets and saw her hands trembling. I sat waiting on a bench, holding my doll, Lila. Strange people were all around us, so I hugged Lila tighter, trying to make her feel better. I watched my mother watch other people going in and out of the bus depot. She was probably searching for any sign of Gene. At one point she was fidgety, so she grabbed my hand and we went to stand right by the door so we could see our bus pull into the station.

Suddenly the bus arrived, brakes wheezing, sliding doors clanking open, luggage loudly unloaded out of the side compartments. Then the bus driver stood in the doorway and called out, "This way folks. Have your tickets ready!" I remember climbing the tall stairs onto the bus, walking down a long aisle past dark rows of seats. I remember that on that first bus, we sat way back so I could lie down on my mother's lap and go to sleep holding Lila. It was dark in the back, and when the bus stopped to pick up other people, my mother would hold me close and tuck us into the hidden corner as if to snuggle with me, but it felt too tight.

As the bus rolled down the highway, I looked up at my mother's face and saw lights from passing highway signs flashing on and off her face. Her eyes were always open; she never slept. I could hear the bus tires droning beneath us, not knowing it was our freedom song. A small floor light cast a soft glow up the aisle so I could see the profiles of other passengers, their heads all nodding in sleep.

If I sat up, I could look out the window at the dark landscape flying by, an occasional yard light casting shadows on buildings, a sign by a gas pump outside a small store. "We just need a couple of days, sweetheart. A couple of days," my mother whispered into the darkness, more to herself than to me. Little did I know that every mile the bus driver put behind us was a gift. For my mother, these miles between Texas and Minnesota may have felt like one of those footbridges suspended over the bayous in the South. When you were on it, you were suspended between two points, but if you fell, there were cottonmouth snakes below and certain death.

I don't know what went through my mother's mind in those first hours as we escaped. I only know that when I opened my eyes, she was often looking at me. At one point she whispered, "You will be safe. By God, whatever I have to do, you will be safe." How can a young child sense conviction in her mother's voice? I did.

Every time the bus slowed down to let someone off the bus, my mother would tense up, go on high alert. She pulled me in tight and tried to make us as small as we could be in the back seat, tucking our heads low. I could hear her holding her breath until the bus driver closed the door again, that great wheezing gulp of air echoing her own sigh of relief as the driver slid the bus into gear and slowly ambled back onto the highway. It was as if that big old bus was cradling us and rocking us to freedom. The longer we rode the bus, I noticed, the more often my mother let her eyes close. She dared some sleep.

Sometimes the bus stopped and we had to get off to get on a different bus, so we bought sandwiches to take with us. At each stop, my mother hesitated before we got off. I watched her look out the windows, check out the crowd of people waiting to board in depots along the way. She was constantly watchful, as if we were being chased, like when you play hide-and-seek and you're trying to get to home base with the tagger right behind you.

I remember odd people we saw at some of the stops. Ladies had their hair in bobby pins with scarves wrapped around their heads. My mother would never go out of the house with bobby pins in her hair, so that was funny to me. Then there was the spooky man who sat in the back of one bus and kept lunging his way down the aisle, muttering bad words. The bus driver suddenly stopped the bus in a small town, stormed to the back, and ordered the spooky man off the bus. That was scary.

By the time we boarded our very last bus on our way to Crosby, my mother invited me to sit in the first seat so I could look out the big window in the front of the bus. I watched the white dash marks move under the bus and saw barns and farmyards along the way. I gazed at the huge lake my mother said was called Lake Mille Lacs. I watched for cows and horses and spotted an occasional dog. The best sight of all was when the bus slowed down and pulled up in front of a store, and a man was standing waiting for us. He wore his work shirt, work pants, suspenders, and billed work cap. "There's your grandpa," my mother said. I had only met him once before.

His face looked serious through the bus window, but he gave us big hugs and a smile when he greeted us. By then it was dusk, and he loaded us into the truck to drive to the farm. My grandmother was waiting for us. "You little sweetheart, you're with Grandma now," she whispered into my ear as she kissed me on each cheek, holding my small face in her hands and burying me in her soft arms next to her chest.

Bed felt good that night. We slept on a soft featherbed under my grandmother's handmade quilts, quilts so heavy I couldn't roll over. During the night, I heard the old telephone ring, a long and two shorts. I heard my grandpa yelling at someone on the telephone. I figured it must be Gene. I could hear Grandpa shouting, "You come near this farm and I will blow your head off, you son of a bitch!" He slammed the phone back on the hook. As he got back into bed with Grandma, my mother and I snuggled closer to each other as Grandpa said something about "murdering the whole family to get her back." I didn't understand all the words, but I knew anger.

The next morning, my grandmother made me sourdough pancakes. After breakfast Grandpa walked me up the driveway. "I want to show you something." He closed a big metal gate and put a lock and chain on it. "Now, you don't go near this gate, you hear? It's really important that you stay up near the house or the barn with the kids. Nothing's going to happen to you. Grandpa and Grandma are going to take care of you. You remember that." When we returned to the house, I watched Grandpa put his shotgun on a rack above the kitchen door.

Gene never showed up.

## 14

# Sanctuary

Those first weeks were very tense. The gate remained locked. The shotgun remained above the front door. As we made trips to the barn, outhouse, clothesline, and woodpile, my grandparents, along with Uncle Dale, Aunt Della, and Uncle Sidney, who were in high school and still lived on the farm, watched the road and the gate. I watched them.

My mother helped Grandpa with chores and Grandma around the house. We settled into a daily routine. Cows needed to be milked, barns cleaned, pigs fed. Water had to be carried from the well over and down the hill, gardens weeded, clothes washed and hung on the line, wood carried in from the woodpile. On the farm if you consumed, you produced, so I learned new chores. For the first time in my young life, each day had a steady rhythm, sameness, constancy.

When weeks passed and Gene didn't show up, my mother relaxed a little and started laughing again. I don't know if I had ever seen my mother laugh really hard, but now I did, and her laughing made me giggle. She began to play practical jokes on Grandpa and on her brothers and sister, which I learned was a Palmer trait. Meanwhile, she and I absorbed a sense of safety and security.

One day, my mother suggested we take a walk out into the pasture, so we climbed under the fence and followed two dirt tracks down the hill to the windmill and troughs where the cows were gathered to drink. Gophers skittered across the grass and into their holes. It felt good to be in open spaces, away from gate watching. We crossed a little creek and climbed a hill covered in trees, wildflowers, and grasses. When we reached the top, down the hill on the other side was another large pasture. All the grass was lying down on the ground.

"What happened?" I asked.

"Grandpa cuts the hay and uses it to feed the cows."

We walked the length of that hill for a while and then saw two dirt tracks that led into the woods.

"Where do these go?" I asked.

"Grandpa uses these paths to take the horses and wagon into the woods to cut down trees. He cuts up the logs and sells them to people." This was a strange new world. "Let's sit down. I need a rest." My mother found us a log to sit on overlooking the distant pasture.

"Honey, I need to talk to you about something. I need to go to Minneapolis to find a job. I need to make money so, eventually, I can rent a place for us to live. We can't stay with Grandma and Grandpa forever."

"That's okay. I'll go with you and help."

"But you have to go to school. You're six years old and haven't started school yet. There's a really good school just up the road not far from here."

"What do you mean?" I was beginning to get worried.

"Grandma and Grandpa want you to stay with them a little longer. Looking for a job and a place to live will be hard. I need to know someone'll take care of you. I think it'd be best if you stayed on the farm and started school. I need to go alone."

"But you won't be here. I'll be alone. I don't know Grandma and Grandpa very well. Or Della or Sidney or Dale." The thought of her leaving was a crushing blow.

"I will visit you on weekends. I promise." Her voice was shaking.

A few days later, Grandpa loaded my mother's suitcase into the truck and we drove into town. Buses did not hold favorable memories for me, but there we were again, watching the big Greyhound pull in. I held my mother tightly, hoping she might change her mind, but after a kiss and a raggedy "I love you—see you real soon," she was swallowed up by the bus's gulping door.

She had left me with strangers before, but this time was different. I was old enough to grasp what was happening. Many nights I cried myself to sleep. The trauma that forced us to the farm haunted me. Night terrors set in. I often woke up screaming. I bit my nails and picked my skin. When my mother called the farm, I begged her to come get me. She wanted to come see me, but she was working, the weather was bad, or she didn't have the money for bus tickets. There were long periods of time between her visits.

It must have been hard on my grandparents to know what to do to give me comfort. One day, my grandpa returned from a trip to town. "Karla, come outside and look in the truck. There's something I want to show you." I followed him outside, and he lifted me up on the bed of the truck. There, in a cage, was a beautiful white rabbit with fuchsia pink eyes.

"This is for you. You'll have to learn to take good care of him. He's your bunny now. He's going to count on you." I had never had a pet. I named him Lucky because I felt lucky to have him and knew he would be lucky to have me. A small white rabbit helped begin to fill a hole in my soul.

Each day I raced to the barn to feed Lucky, hold him, stroke him, talk to him, tell him all the things I couldn't tell anyone else. He was warm and soft, and he stayed close. After a few weeks, I began to take him out in the farmyard so he could nibble on the grass and we could sit in the sunshine. Those were some of my happiest days during that time.

Then it happened. One afternoon I didn't have any chores, so I decided to let Lucky out of his cage. I sat in the grass watching him twitch his nose and move about cautiously. My grandfather was working on the tractor in the yard. My grandmother was hanging clothes on the line. My aunt and uncles were doing their own chores.

Then out of nowhere, a flash! I barely saw him out of the corner of my eye. Skipper, the farm dog, was racing toward me. In an instant he grabbed Lucky by the head and shook him violently, then dropped him to the ground. I don't remember what happened next, except I could hear myself screaming. My grandparents shouted my name. My aunt and uncles came running. I remember picking Lucky off the ground and laying him across my lap. He was completely limp. I watched foam seep out of his mouth and watched his eyes turn from pink to white. The pink eyes turning white became my nightmare for weeks.

Grandma cradled me, rocking me back and forth as I cradled Lucky for as long as it took me to get my breath again. "I am so sorry. I am so sorry," was all I could hear her saying in my ear. At some point I pulled back and looked at my grandma. "What do we do?" Death was a way of life on the farm, as animals were raised for food, slaughtered, and set on the table, but my grandmother was looking into the eyes of a child who knew nothing of that. "Well, when those we love die, we have a funeral. We need to give Lucky a proper burial." I wasn't sure what she was talking about, but I listened. "First, we need to put Lucky in a box, and I have the perfect thing. I'll be right back."

Grandma returned from the house with a girdle box from Sears and Roebuck. She gently picked Lucky up from my lap and carefully laid him in the box. He fit perfectly.

By now, Della, Sidney, and Dale had joined us. "Come with me, kids." Grandma took me by the hand and, carrying the box, led all of us down the hill behind the outhouse to a little level patch of grass next to a stand of birch trees. "I think this is a nice spot. What do you think, Karla? Dale, why don't you go get the shovel."

In minutes my grandma, dressed in her housedress and calico apron, began to dig a hole. My aunt and uncles moved the dirt around with their hands. Once she was done, my grandma laid the box in the hole, and we all took dirt in our hands and dropped some on the box. All of a sudden, Della said, "Wait, we need a gravestone." She and Sidney searched among the trees and emerged with a big rock, and she scratched Lucky's name on it. "Shall we say a prayer?" Grandma asked. We all bowed our heads.

I learned something about earth to earth, ashes to ashes, and dust to dust that day that I couldn't begin to understand. We decided the grave needed more decoration. We found tiny rocks in the driveway, circled the grave with small stones, and then wrote Lucky's name with rocks. Della picked some columbine in the woods and laid it on the grave. Something about that burial gave me a sense of place. I knew where Lucky would always be. I didn't always know where my mother was, but I knew where this family was, that they were there for me.

Years later, a friend asked me whether violence was a part of my mother's family, if this was how my mother and my aunt ended up in violent relationships. I explained that violence wasn't part of our family but insidiously entered it, stole its way in through the naïveté of two sisters. They were far from home, far from their family and the safety of relatives. They were subsumed by seductive men, who, like the farm dog, waited for the moment to strike. Those men tried to steal the life right out of my mother and my aunt. They didn't succeed.

# 15

# An Alleviation

## *Box 136, Little Pine Route*

"Grandma, I'm scared to go to school."

"Well, that's understandable, but I think you'll like it once you get there," my grandmother replied to me in her soothing voice.

"Who'll be there?"

"Other kids in the township who take the school bus, just like you."

"Who'll help Grandpa in the garage? I just want to stay home and eat pie with Grandpa after chores."

"I know you do. Grandpa will miss you too. But I packed you a good lunch to take to school."

"But who'll help Dale clean the barn?"

"You have another job now. It's to go to school just like Della and Sidney. They take the school bus, too."

"Will you come with me?"

"I sure will, honey. I can come with you to the bus today. But most days, Dale will walk with you."

This was how my grandmother planted me in school for the first time in my life. That morning, she took my hand and walked me up the dirt driveway to the road. We were a quirky threesome as we waddled along: Grandma in her housedress and calico apron, me carrying my lunch pail, and Dale tagging along behind, wearing his red-and-black-plaid billed cap. I looked back over my shoulder at the farmhouse, and there was

Grandpa waving goodbye. I knew he was going to miss me as much as I would miss him.

When we climbed the last hill, Grandma instructed me on what to do.

"You have to be sure to cross the road and stand by the mailbox because the bus will be coming from that way." She pointed to the right down the road. "Now, if you wait and wait and the bus doesn't come, it might mean that you missed the bus. If that happens, then you come back to the house, and Dale will pull you in the wagon or on the sled. It isn't too far."

Indeed, later there were times when I missed the bus, and Dale wasn't too happy about being my transport to school, especially in the winter. He groused at me all the way in his harmless, grumpy manner.

That day, the orange school bus motored down the road and stopped by our mailbox. The driver greeted me with a big smile and a "Good morning! Is this our new student?"

Grandma helped me up the stairs and onto the bus, promising, "I'll be right here waiting for you when you come home today. Don't you worry." I saw other kids on the bus but sat down in the first seat I could find, then peered out the window to see Grandma and Dale wave at me as we pulled away. This was the second scariest bus ride of my life.

Soon I saw a white clapboard building on the right side of the road, surrounded by a large clearing and with a small building in the yard that looked like an outhouse. As I climbed the stairs to the schoolhouse, I looked at the woman standing in the doorway welcoming us. This was the teacher, Miss Hite. She had a nice smile. I soon learned she and I were both born on Abraham Lincoln's birthday, which made me feel special.

The schoolhouse had two big rooms. One was empty except for benches that lined the walls. When it wasn't being used for playtime on stormy or bitter cold days, it served as a community meeting room and a venue for wedding dances for people in the township. The other room was lined with bookshelves filled with a smattering of books. There were six rows of desks in the middle of the room, and each row represented a grade. I sat in the first row and later learned the other two kids in first grade were my distant cousins.

It was a year of navigating. I got to know kids, learned new games, and dodged porcupines in the outhouse. It was a year of discovering the world of words, paragraphs, chapters, and numbers. I loved books, and once I honed my reading skills, I burrowed my way through every book in the small school library.

It was my grandmother who gave me back my childhood. She wanted each day filled with life, not fear, as she strived to heal the impact of the Greyhound bus ride, terrifying phone calls, threats to the family, a shotgun above the farmhouse door, and a locked farm gate. She held me when I woke up in the night from bad dreams; her soft arms pushed the scary memories back as she whispered hushed words of comfort. It was Grandma who believed in the importance of my sitting down at the dinner table every night and looking into the faces of people who loved me. She also knew what I needed to hold my world together: love, purpose, and an opportunity to contribute, which meant work on the farm. She loved me all the while she taught me to churn butter, shuck peas, pull homemade taffy, and clean berries. She loved me as I balked at hoeing onions, beans, and potatoes in the garden in the hot midday sun. She loved me when I whined on my way out the door, bundled up in my winter jacket, with my tiny water pails—made by my grandpa out of Karo syrup cans with wire handles—headed to the well with Dale to fetch water.

She showed me that the animals were our food as she held a chicken by the feet with one hand and chopped its head off with the other. She had Dale teach me how to carry wood from the woodpile to the wood box, how to clean barns, and how to feed corn to the pigs. Even after I moved to Minneapolis with my mother, I lived with my grandparents on the farm every summer until I was hired for my first summer job in high school.

Over those years, I learned that the families in the township knew my grandmother's kindness, her ethic of being your brother and sister's keeper, her devotion to her husband and family. They knew that she rose each day with a covenant on her heart to make her garden produce food for her family and make her simple house a home. I listened and learned how she and my grandfather settled first into an old house that was already on this plot of land. In time it rotted away board by board, too drafty and cold for babies, so my grandfather dug and built a basement foundation.

This hole in the ground became my grandmother's dream for a new, warm house that wouldn't be a reality for many years.

When my grandmother moved into that basement it had concrete-block walls, a cement floor, and a wire strung across one end to create curtained bedrooms. The wood-burning heating stove, made from an oil barrel, sat in the center of the basement, with the kitchen table and wood-burning cookstove on one side and a dining room table, buffet, and treadle sewing machine on the other. The latter's drawers brimmed with buttons for entertaining children and eventually grandchildren.

She wasn't a proud woman, but her pleasure was a pantry filled with canned goods put up from her garden, where she raised swiss chard, radishes, onions, cucumbers, potatoes, and beets. We would all go into the woods with my grandmother for days at a time to pick chokecherries, raspberries, and blueberries for making jam. She made lard from pork fat and churned butter from the cream that rose to the top of the milk pail. She kept her family clean: catching rain from the eaves in copper boilers, heating the water on top of the wood-burning stove, washing clothes in a large pot, and then wringing them through a hand-turned wringer. Her children said their bedtime prayers and slept under heavy homemade quilts created from patches of old work clothes. "Good morning, merry sunshine," was her daily greeting as she coaxed children and later grandchildren from bed into morning chores that needed to be done before catching the bus to school. She moved through her rituals, stitching together the life of her family.

At the close of day, my grandmother gathered her family around the square, Formica-topped kitchen table flooded with amber light from the kerosene lantern hanging overhead. As each of us came in from our chores of milking cows, gathering firewood, or repairing an engine in the garage, we stomped our feet to mark the transition to the table. We cleared cow dung, snow, wood chips, and sawdust off our shoes. We cast our jackets onto hooks on the wall. We made our way to the table, the smell of supper luring each of us to our usual chair, the incense of our daily meal inviting us to rest, break bread, take, eat. *This is the body given for you.*

This table held this family for a lifetime of children, grandchildren, and great-grandchildren. It held cups of coffee and pieces of pie to welcome neighbors who dropped in. It welcomed sorrow and solace for a meal after a burial, and, years later, it held the worry of the family at the end of the trial each day, returning from the courthouse not knowing what the next day might bring. This small congregation of family listened, laughed, and learned with respect, reverence, and maybe a little fear. All of this was ours to wade through, to hold, endure, and, hopefully, overcome. We learned that all of this life was something to be thankful for, even the hard parts, because it was still a life lived.

It was in the kitchen where my grandmother reigned. It was at her kitchen table that she gathered her congregation of family, prayed, and offered gratitude for God's protection and blessing. Prayer was new to me, so I was fascinated that everyone closed their eyes, but I peeked to watch my grandmother's face soften as she bowed her head. "Heavenly Father, bless these, thy gifts, which we are about to receive from thy bounty, bless them to our needs, through Christ, Our Lord. Amen." Each word was intentional, weighted with reverence in hushed gratitude for months of work—feeding, milking, slaughtering, planting, and sowing—that were a part of the simple meal before us. I loved watching my grandma pray, her face lit only by kerosene lamplight.

When we first lived with my grandparents, I had not yet been to church, but I now know that church was experienced at that table. When church was too far a drive due to bad weather or when gas was scarce, the roads were washed out, or hay needed to be mowed that day, communion was at that table. For my grandmother, this was the body, her family. It was here that she tended wounds and brought comfort with mashed potatoes and gravy, fried salted pork, and a good piece of pie. It was here, in my childhood and throughout the years, she cared for her children and grandchildren and helped them bear the crosses of their lives and choices. At age six, I began to learn this while peeking through prayer.

With "Amen," everyone began devouring their supper with small talk of weather or what went well: "That new engine part slid right into place. Damn, I like it when that happens!" Or what went wrong: "Brownie and Big Red went at it again in the barn as I was trying to get them into their stanchions. Had to break them up. That bad blood between those cows probably won't get resolved until one of them becomes a pot roast."

I listened as Grandpa preached on the injustice of the poor prices the creamery was paying local farmers for their milk. "Fear not," he declared, the Democratic-Farmer-Labor Party would rise again after Eisenhower.

I watched and listened to all of this as a wide-eyed little girl coming to know her family. In time I learned there was a promise at that table that no matter what life delivered, this family would gather there and warm our hands with one another. I had never known family before. I was learning that it was the ground of my being, our being. Seasons would come and go, raspberries would be picked over, holiday piecrust rolled out, and pigs would be slaughtered in the spring, but always a prayer would be issued to the good Lord to bless us, keep us all safe, and remind us that glad hearts are still possible, even in the dark dusk of day. It was on a Formica-topped table that I learned communion and breaking bread.

Years later, as a pastor, I invited others to the communion table with these words: "Come not because you must, but because you may. All are welcome. Please come." I deeply treasure celebrating the Lord's table, for it was at my grandmother's table that I first planted the seeds of my faith and experienced the presence of something greater than our small selves, embodied in a family's love and compassion.

# 16

## A Blessing

I was hypervigilant and tentative with my grandfather at first. In those first forty-eight hours, my six-year-old eyes searched him, watched his every move, listened to his words to determine if he was safe. I watched his hands as they tugged on the bill of his cap, opened barn doors, lifted a pitchfork, or gestured as he spoke. I watched for angry hands, but I didn't see them. I listened to the tone of his voice, loud or soft, gentle or harsh, but I never heard it loud or harsh. I was watchful, gathering information.

I was a little girl who had lived with a man who was not safe. As hungry as I was for a father and male affection, my grandfather underwent intense scrutiny.

Even though he said the words, "Don't go near the gate. Grandpa is going to take care of you," I had to experience that he meant it. I had heard that promise. "You come near this farm and I will blow your head off, you son of a bitch." Looking into my grandfather's craggy face and crinkly Irish eyes, I came to know the truth. He would protect me. The shotgun on the rack above the kitchen door did not escape me. This was part of my watchfulness, the constant vigilance, gathering in every important detail. If I paid close enough attention, I might be safe.

In time, I learned to trust him. I adored Grandpa and became his shadow. I wanted to be like him, so I wore his huge work boots, plopped the linings of his old hats on my head, and toddled after him as he did his chores. He was the first man who seemed to cherish me, and he imprinted that on me like a mother duckling does her baby. I followed him everywhere. As he worked, he talked to me, telling me stories, almost as if he wanted me to understand this family and its history.

He told me that the school I went to had served as the Ross Lake town hall and community center for years. "Your grandma and I had only been married for a couple years when we first drove here on two dirt trails in 1927. There were only a hundred or so folks who lived back in here. The land had been logged over once, but a second growth made it promising to men like me who wanted to do a little logging. And you know that mining pit we pass on the way to town? The town was named after George Crosby, who hoped the iron ore business would make this a big metropolis on the Cuyuna Range. Yes, those years were tough years, but good years."

Sometimes he seemed lost in his memories. "Yeah, we drove down into this property, saw the hardwoods and birch, acres of meadows—though they had loads of rock in them. It sure wasn't good land for farming, but it was beautiful. We could only afford one well, so we had to put it down in the pasture for the cows. Too bad, because we've hauled water up to the house for years. Thank God for you kids! And thank God for Doc and Tony. They're bigger than the Budweiser horses. Did you know that? They helped me haul logs out of the woods so I could run them through my sawmill and sell the lumber. Yup, that's how we got started. That and a couple dairy cows." I listened to Grandpa, hanging on every word. "Your grandma and I had a dream, and this land was a big part of it." He was proud of what he had accomplished.

Sometimes he laughed over the practical jokes he liked to play on his kids and grandkids. I wasn't going to escape his Irish humor if I wanted to be a full-fledged member of the family. Not long after I arrived on the farm, he urged me to go ask Grandma for a "left-handed monkey wrench." When I came back, telling him I couldn't find one, he sent me to the barn to ask my uncle Sidney for a "sky hook." I suspect he chuckled the entire time I wandered around the farm, searching out these tools. One day, my grandpa dug a hole in the yard and then called me over and asked me, "Do you want to help Grandpa?" I was anxious to please, so he handed me the posthole digger. "Could you please move this hole over about three feet?" He marked a line in the sand with his foot so I would know where the hole should go. My grandfather, aunt, and uncles stood over behind the garage and cackled while I stood there contemplating the hole, trying to figure out how to do the job I had been asked to do. I would put the posthole digger in the empty space, pinch hard, and come up with only air. I did this several times before Grandpa came and rescued me. It also wasn't beyond him to arrange a snipe hunt for gullible grandkids. One evening, Dale and I sat on the edge of a marsh, holding gunnysacks open and whistling for snipe, waiting for those birds to dash into our bags. After enough bug bites, even I figured out we had been tricked.

These were rites of passage to be welcomed into the family. Grandpa loved to tease, and he always told me I had freckles because I "stood too close behind a cow" or I had brown eyes because I was "full up to here" as he placed his hand above his eyebrows. I didn't always understand the jokes, but it felt good to be included in the fun.

I trailed my grandfather all over the farm, watching him cut timber, run the sawmill, and work on his equipment. I started to mimic his cussing when he was irritated with the cows or unhappy with a piece of farm equipment. Then my mother, on one of her visits, told Grandpa, "Daddy, you can't be teaching her to talk like that. She has to go to school, and her teacher will have a fit if she talks like that." Grandpa listened very seriously, then winked at me. Even when he was busy, he would tousle my hair and, in the evenings, invite me into his lap. "Come to Grandpa," he would say, and he'd cuddle me in his arms.

Grandpa was playful and loved baseball, acquiring the name Riley on area ball teams. On Sunday afternoons he insisted that the whole family, as well as a few neighbors, stop all work and rustle up a softball game in the farmyard. On a beautiful summer day, under the maple trees, with the wind blowing across the vegetable garden, the kids would be positioned on rocks for bases. He even cajoled Grandma into taking up the bat. "Come on, Ma, knock it out of the ballpark!" Grandma would stand at home plate in her housedress and apron with the bat in her hand, smiling her winsome smile, still loving her husband even when he gave her a hard time.

As neighbors and family came and went, I saw folks in the township turn to my grandfather because he could fix or build anything. If he didn't have a part for a repair, he made it out of old metal. He could mend anything that broke down. In the early days, it was the harnesses on the draft horses; later, his John Deere tractor. When he and Grandma were going to make maple syrup, he built four-by-eight-foot metal cooking pans. They gathered the maple sap in cream cans, poured it into the pans over wood fires, and cooked it down for days into a rich syrup.

As I listened, I learned more about the Irish side of my grandfather. He was known to be a passionate man with a twinkle in his eye, a man who would cuss and carry on about the rigid rules of traditional religion and any politician who wasn't a Democrat, but if anyone in the area needed a helping hand, no matter who they were, Grandpa was there to help. He employed Fred Hassler, a local Ojibwe man who needed work and housing, to help in the sawmill. Fred lived in a small trailer positioned out behind the woodpile in the farmyard, and Grandma invited him into the house for dinner after days of hard work in the woods. My grandfather could not have made it without Fred's help.

Over the years, my grandparents raised seven children on the farm, and eventually more than twenty grandchildren arrived. My grandfather drove the school bus for Aitkin High School to augment his income from sawing lumber in his mill, building sawmills, and selling milk at the Aitkin Creamery. He and my grandmother were determined, with God's help, to make this land provide for their family and the dairy herd. Together, they kept faith with one another, their family, and the land. Together, they were a blessing to a small child.

# 17

## Resurrection

### *1953*

Starting life over wasn't easy for my mother, a young single woman with a child, but she had a deep reservoir of longing and hope inside her. It wasn't in her Palmer genes to become bitter, so instead she let that longing bloom into a new life for us both.

Once she had found a job, she rented one room on the third floor of a rooming house on Twenty-Sixth and Irving Avenue South and moved me to Minneapolis. I was happy to be with my mother again, but mostly I remember walking around in my stocking feet, worrying about disturbing the family who lived downstairs. Our one room served as living room and bedroom. We shared a kitchen and bathroom with another person who lived on the third floor. After the open spaces of the farm, the tiny room was a huge adjustment for an active girl, but moving to that rooming house planted us in a neighborhood that I would love and live in for the rest of my life.

My mother enrolled me in Douglas Elementary School. This was a big change from the one-room schoolhouse in the country. Because I had started school late, my country teacher, Miss Hite, had suggested I skip second grade so I could catch up with my age group. So I began third grade at Douglas, which meant lots of kids, a walk to school, and many adjustments.

Having laid down her burdens, my mother left her old life behind and set to work living a new life. With each new job and small salary increase, she suggested I look in the newspaper for a new apartment for us to rent. I always kept us in my school's neighborhood so I could stay with my friends. Little did I know that as I selected each apartment, I was also creating the canvas for my mother's resurrection and creativity.

My mother had traveled light but carried volumes of beauty inside her. She had meager earnings but a wealth of imagination and talent. As I grew older and made friends, they thought my mother had flair, was playful and fun. Being single, she wasn't in the same spot as the mothers who were weighed down by alcoholic husbands, deadbeat dads, or angry men.

My mother had longed to be an interior decorator, and each cheap apartment we rented became a page in her portfolio. Her resurrected spirit drove her to create beauty wherever she could out of what she had. She loved to say that we had "champagne taste and a beer salary." Plastic flowers, ivy, and ferns were on the cutting edge in the 1950s, and plastic plants sprouted all over our house. They hung in a fake copper teapot on the kitchen wall, spewed out of a cornucopia on the dining room table, filled the back of a sinister-looking ceramic black panther with green rhinestone eyes that sat between the rabbit ears on the television set in our living room. They flowed out of a metallic plastic planter on the back of the toilet. It was a single working mother's garden in a cheap one-bedroom apartment. I remember our kitchen sink filled with dusty plastic plants drenched in soapsuds.

I didn't know my mother was an artist until I was ten years old. We moved to a grand Tudor mansion next door to Hennepin Avenue United Methodist Church, where the church parking lot is now located. We had a small living room, kitchen, and one bedroom, and we shared the bathroom down the hall with a neighbor. The apartment had a fireplace and a bay window, but my mother wanted a view. I watched her as she studied one large, bare wall in the living room. One day, off she went to the hardware store and returned with cans of paint and contact paper. When she finished work each day, the artist went to work. First, she created a wall by placing contact paper that simulated stone below the chair rail. Then she opened cans of paint and began painting her view, including snow-covered mountain peaks, a river, pine trees, and meadow flowers, all reminiscent of calendar art. When it was finished a few days later, she knew it was very good. She sat on the white Naugahyde sofa she'd found at a garage sale, smoked a cigarette, had a cup of coffee, and enjoyed her mountain view.

Not long after that vista was completed, we traded that apartment for a larger basement apartment in the same house that had its own bathroom but needed a face-lift. This time we went to the paint store together, but discovered that the only colors of paint on sale were blue and white. In no time she transformed that gloomy space into a garden-level sky with a light blue living room, a medium blue kitchen, and a deeper blue bedroom. We slept in the night sky together, talking over a matchstick-shade room divider, saying our good nights. It was the first time my mother and I didn't sleep in the same bed. I was thirteen.

My mother's artistic talent also spilled over to fashion. She proclaimed herself a "sewer," not a seamstress. She loved nice clothes, so she frequented a place she called the Paris Shop, one of the earliest consignment stores near downtown by Loring Park. Late at night she would take apart beautiful suits made from fine fabric, then sew them back together, smoking as she worked, her head bent over her Singer sewing machine. The bright light from the machine lit her face, turning her into an intense fashion designer as she updated old trends, improved upon a style, and reworked a suit to fit.

I was fifteen years old before I owned store-bought clothes. My mother spun her fashion magic for me out of necessity. Our family photo album is her fashion portfolio: me at age four in a highly starched, snow-white pinafore worn on Easter Sunday with a white hat, white gloves, and white patent leather shoes; me in a blue polished-cotton dress worn to a sixth-grade boy-girl party; me on the night of my senior prom in a long, blue, raw-silk dress with a pearl-beaded bodice that we tried to make look like Audrey Hepburn's in the movie *Breakfast at Tiffany's*; me in a white wool formal trimmed in light blue ribbon for the University of Minnesota Welcome Week Queen contest.

My mother never used a pattern—she just cut. I would call in the morning to say I needed a dress, and by that night she had pieced it together. I was grateful when I graduated to sleeveless formals because my mother never mastered making sleeves and armholes. I think I was fifteen years old before I knew my arms went all the way down to my sides!

Life was a rhythm and a good beat for my mother, who loved music and loved to dance. A piano invited her untrained fingers to dance along the keys as she played Glenn Miller's "In the Mood" by ear. Music couldn't be contained in her fingers and poured into her entire body. With an occasional bonus at work or a discount coupon, she followed her dance gurus Kathryn and Arthur Murray at a local studio to learn the tango, samba, rumba, and cha-cha. At home, she put on seventy-eight-speed records and we danced in our shorty pajamas—my mother, my friends, and I swirling around our living room, our own starlit ballroom. I was an accomplished ballroom dancer in grade school thanks to Kathryn, Arthur, and my mom.

Sometimes we sang as we danced. My mother loved country western music after living in Houston. Her yodel competed with Patsy Cline's. As a little girl in Texas, I remember sitting on a picnic blanket and eating popcorn while watching Hank Snow movies projected on the brick wall of a neighboring apartment building. We sang along with Hank as he rode his horse across the prairie. Our taste in music was unusual when we first arrived in Minnesota, but that didn't stop us. My mother acted as if she were auditioning for *Arthur Godfrey's Talent Scouts* as she belted out songs while she cleaned house or as we rode in the car to my grandparents' farm. We sang honky-tonk tunes and old songs like "Goodnight, Irene," "Beautiful Brown Eyes," or Christmas carols on the Fourth of July. A hairbrush became a microphone, and we were on stage, starring on the television show *Your Hit Parade*.

When my mother died very unexpectedly on New Year's Eve in 1975, I was twenty-nine years old and single. Cleaning out her apartment alone was my daunting responsibility. On the morning I planned to begin, two old high school friends I had not spoken to in many years, Susan Jacox and Linda Sundell, called unexpectedly to express their sympathy. When I told them my packing plan for the day, they asked if they could help.

Sue and Linda had often shared my mother's company over a cup of coffee at our house while I was out on a date. I would come home, and there would be my mother with my friends, laughing around the kitchen table with plastic flowers as the centerpiece. It was my mother's plastic Garden of Gethsemane, where kids took refuge as she listened and remained awake late into the night, however long it took to ease the pain or laugh them into their lighter selves.

When Sue, Linda, and I arrived at my mother's apartment, I organized my thoughts while my friends toured her apartment with quiet reverence. In time, they spotted some of my mother's treasures that verged on kitsch, reminding them of familiar times in our home and the great laughs we'd had in the past over my mother's finds. Each discovery on their tour brought sweet smiles and, eventually, marvelous belly laughs as we reminisced. It was a lovely and fitting wake.

Because my mother died during the holiday season, her apartment was still festooned with Christmas decorations. We packed away my mother's artificial Christmas tree, unscrewing it branch by branch after removing plastic ornaments, sprayed white flowers, a few holiday cards, and lights. The fake tree smelled faintly like a real tree as we disassembled it. Then we found the pine-scented car deodorizer buried deep in the branches. There were the three angels with a few feathers for hair. (My children now love these angels; every year, as they emerge from the decorations box, I tell the story of my mother loving them so much.) Then we put away the crèche, which I bought at age fifteen when my mother gave me fifteen dollars to buy new ornaments for our tree. When I arrived at Dayton's, I fell in love with the crèche and decided that Mary, Joseph, Baby Jesus, and all the shepherds, wise men, and animals were worth a few more years of sprayed flowers and plastic ornaments.

My old friends and I spread out through my mother's apartment, packing up her art collection. There was a red Japanese lantern with colorful fringes and another lamp that, when it was turned on, warmed up an inside cylinder that revolved, giving the illusion of a moving waterfall and a flowing stream. In the bathroom was the framed cardboard hologram of Michelangelo's *Pietà*. In her bedroom we found the very Nordic-looking portrait of Jesus, with hair that always reminded me of the Breck Shampoo girls on television. We found the hammered-copper image of the Last Supper. I kept it packed away for years, but now it holds a place of honor above the refrigerator in our seventy-year-old cabin in northwestern

Wisconsin, watching over and blessing all of our family meals. My mother would love how its copper reflects the golden knotty-pine walls. She would be pleased at the new significance her rare art now holds in my life's work.

Remembering my mother's artistic expression reminds me of a lovely paraphrased passage from the Gospel According to Thomas: "If you bring forth what is within you, what is within you will save you. If you do not bring forth what is within you, what is within you will destroy you" (Saying 70).

My mother was not about to be destroyed. Her creative spirit was her salvation. Her physical poverty was liberated by it. As she experienced many small deaths in her life, she forged her own small and resounding resurrections. She painted what she knew—calendar art. She sang from what she heard—the radio. She danced from what she experienced—discounted dance coupons. She designed her own fashion creations from other people's cast-off clothes. She created with her own eye from a life force greater than her own life's proportion. She dazzled her daughter with her boldness and daring, her freedom and vitality. As she resurrected herself, she showed me how to reach for new life as well.

As I've danced with my own children, painted watercolors with them in an old rowboat on the lake, sung in the car on trips to the cabin, painted dead fish prints on T-shirts, and collaborated with my kids to transform old pieces of junk into reused furniture, my mother's spirit carries on. As I have watched my daughter take beautiful photographs, prepare her own baby's room with artistic touches, and create imaginative Halloween costumes, my mother's creativity echoes, mother to daughter to granddaughter. As I watch my son exercise his photographer's eye, crafting his own creative work into a career, my mother's art, which saved her, endures. Even without my children ever knowing their grandmother, this is her legacy.

# 18

## Strong Girl

### 1955

It wasn't clear to me why we moved to Albert Lea. I asked questions, but there weren't clear answers or easy explanations. We were settled in Minneapolis, though the rooming house wasn't ideal. Then, suddenly, we moved. I didn't know why.

Years later, while going through my mother's papers, I found something that answered my question: a divorce certificate from Albert Lea dated 1955. I discovered my mother had never legally divorced Charles, the man whose name was on my birth certificate. More secrets.

In the 1950s, births, marriages, and divorces were published in the local newspaper. My mother wanted to get divorced, but she didn't want her family or friends to know she had been legally married to Charles all those years, especially when she had led her family to believe she was married to Gene. So off we went.

We moved into 816 West Clark Street, a little story-and-a-half white clapboard house with a small yard. A single mother with one child was an oddity, but our landlord and landlady, along with their son, Dickie, didn't seem to care. Dickie was the first boy I ever knew who had a Mohawk haircut, and a blond one at that. We were both only children, and we bonded as playmates.

My mother worked at the Wilson meat packing plant in the daytime, was a hostess at the Hotel Albert cocktail lounge at night, and sold Avon products in her spare time. Helen and Elmer took care of me when my mother was at work, adding to a long list of Helens and Elmers who watched over me through those years of no daycare programs.

They reminded me of Jack Sprat and his wife. She was round and red-faced, while he was long and tall. He was a serious man who had long lines in his face that mirrored his body shape. Occasionally he would rise from his recliner, leave the television, and go to the bathroom. This was the full extent of his activity. He would emerge to return to his recliner, but he couldn't even seem to do this with complete success. There he stood, rumpled and wrinkled, looking half asleep; everything about him drooped, even his fly. Either from the effect of a few beers or not caring, all was seldom back in its proper place. I had already learned to be watchful, so even as a girl, my eyes would dart to do a quick check and sure enough, Elmer would have missed again.

I was scared to death the cow really would come out of the barn, as I had heard my grandpa say to my uncles when he told them to check their flies. It was amazing how a fly could take on such magnitude, fill the entire house, and compel me upstairs or outside to play. It took only one glance; then I was terrified and gone.

There weren't any girls on my block, so it just seemed natural to play with the boys in my immediate neighborhood. Dickie didn't seem to be a popular kid, but he was my entry into the tight little group of boys. Arnold and Ray, the police officer's kids, had a complete playhouse in their backyard. We liked to use it as our hideout and lookout post, from which we watched the house across the alley as dusk turned to dark. A young couple lived upstairs, and we somehow thought there was great mystery in peeping on them through the second-floor bathroom window. We saw a lot of teeth get brushed, mouthwash get gargled, and hair get combed, and not much mystery.

Gary's dad owned the small neighborhood grocery store next door to our house. It sold penny candy and basic necessities, and had a meat counter. One day, we cowboys dismounted our horses, parked them in the bike rack outside the store, and piled into the store for candy. We walked into a sight to beat all sights. There was a lady bending over and looking into the meat counter. On her last bathroom stop, she had accidentally tucked her skirt inside her girdle and there it was, her behind in all its glory. We saw London and France, garters, hose, and big pink thighs. The cowboys beat it out of Dodge City fast, hootin' and hollerin' as we pedaled all the way around the block, laughing our heads off.

Mark, Billie, and Hal lived on the other side of the block, a short bike ride. Clyde lived over the tracks in a big house with two stories. Sometimes we couldn't get to Clyde's house because the trains would pause on the track, hitching and unhitching railroad cars for what seemed like hours. Big brown boxcars blocked our way, a great canyon we couldn't cross. We had heard a story of a boy who tried to cross the tracks by crawling under the cars and got run over by a train. This scared us half to death, so the closest we ever got to the trains was sliding pennies onto the track and then running as fast as we could go, terrified a train might come.

Four of us would walk to school together, pick up Clyde, and make our way to Lincoln Elementary School. I took pride in going to Lincoln School because I was born on Abraham Lincoln's birthday. Since it was a national holiday, I got the day off from school, which made me the envy of my small gang. But once I walked onto the schoolyard, something happened. Being a girl descended upon me, and I found myself relegated to jumping rope with the girls instead of playing dodgeball with my friends. The girls also had to play little plastic flutophones in music class, while the boys got the big brass instruments. On the playground, the boys put worms down the girls' blouses. So, by virtue of my gender, I played a wimpy instrument and fended off nightcrawlers by day. It was my first lesson in gender inequity.

Once the school bell rang, the boys and I crossed the tracks and became a cavalry again, a living posse to be reckoned with. We headed for the open prairie to mount our horses, stalk Indians, shoot robbers and outlaws, and cause the townspeople trouble. Occasionally, two girls, Leann and Kendra, invited me to play with them. They lived two blocks away, and their favorite game was to watch the soap opera called *Love of Life* on television. After watching the half-hour show, we took turns acting out the parts of Bruce and Vanessa as they coped with divorce, multiple marriages, alcoholism, love affairs, and intrigue. But for me, it wasn't a game—it was too close to real life. I gladly returned to the refuge of the open plains and high adventure with the boys.

That was the year I learned to feel strong in this boy world, to be able to play on a team, to discover I could hold my own. I tested the limits of my young body, feeling powerful when I had felt so powerless. I learned how to pedal fast, climb trees, scale onto garage roofs, and place cardboard in my bike wheels so it sounded like a motorbike when I was cruising along. We used water balloons and peashooters as weapons against perceived enemies, but the slingshot was my weapon of choice, and I was a sharpshooter. I was a spy, outlaw, cowboy, Superman, all rolled into one. I shot my arrows, aimed my bullets, leaped tall buildings with a single bound, lived in a world of adventure. My body, heart, and spirit were fueled by imagination, strength, power, and accepting pals.

One night, Dickie and I broke the windshield of a passing car shooting acorns with our slingshots. The man's car came to a screeching halt. We ran. There was hell to pay, but the jail term, timeout, dissipated with the next day's sunlight and frontiers to conquer. We rode pretend horses and pressed our bellies to every inch of concrete on the block as if we were marines in the Battle of Pork Chop Hill. It was a marvelous year, a free year, an empowering year.

But in the deep, dark quiet of my sun-porch bedroom, I lay in bed and pondered this new world I had created for myself. I felt something else was at hand in making my life just a bit better. Above my bed, keeping me company, was a glow-in-the-dark Jesus. This was my award for attending vacation Bible school with Dickie the previous summer. Quiet, peaceful, his calm and gentle face lighting up the tiny room, Jesus was suspended there on the wall, a different kind of friend, companion, pal. I thought he was God. I had heard my grandmother pray to God, so I figured this must be him. In the dark I was comforted by this buddy on the wall; there was an integration of my powerful daytime life and my nighttime vulnerabilities. I can't name a moment of crossing over, but cross over I did. I crossed over into my own strength, knowing that what had happened to me up to that point in my life was not right. I wanted to continue feeling strong.

Somehow, even at age nine, I knew that as I was learning to extend my body and reach into the branches of the highest tree, I was also learning an inside power, strength, and resolve that went down deep inside me. I don't know how I knew this. I just felt it. Out of that sense of strength came a resolve to make my life better. Though I didn't have the words, I could feel a righteous indignation over what had happened to me. I fell asleep each night still a bit scared, but stronger, saying thank you to that glow-in-the-dark Jesus on the wall while I waited for my mother to return home from work. I could hear her climb the stairs tired at the end of a long day, having worked two jobs. She always came to my bed, gave me a kiss, and whispered, "I love you, my little Sugarfoot." Glow-in-the dark Jesus watched over us.

## Part 4

## My Choice: Getting from There to Here

We had come so far from where we started, and weren't nearly approaching where we had to be, but we were on the road to becoming better.

—Maya Angelou, *A Song Flung Up to Heaven*

# 19

## Wildly Lucky

### *1961*

We lived in Albert Lea only one year, but just long enough for my mother to secretly secure her divorce. As a nine-year old, I was unaware that my mother was dealing with legal issues while balancing three jobs and me. Once she knew the divorce was final, she packed us up and we moved back to the same familiar neighborhood in Minneapolis. I returned to Douglas Grade School and my friends, somehow knowing not to ask many questions. I just felt lucky at the time. And then a few years later, the murder happened and then the trial.

As a thirteen-year-old girl, I had no idea what I needed to do to come home to my body, mind, and spirit after my aunt Lila's trial. Junior high school in Minneapolis was to be lived through, and I made it. I made it through mean girls, slam books, and cliques with a few close friends I loved and trusted. Together we used peroxide on our hair; Scotch-taped our bangs; used Man Tan, a product guaranteed to make us look like bronze goddesses; cut our hair into pixie haircuts; bought Capezio flats; watched Justine and Bob do the slow dancing on *American Bandstand*; and swooned at slumber parties when Frankie Avalon sang about girls exchanging bobby socks for stockings and their toys for boyfriends. But none of my peers knew I had made it through murder.

Two years later, I was a scrawny, freckled fifteen-year-old when I entered West High School in Minneapolis in the fall of 1961. I carried my family secret into a school of tenth, eleventh, and twelfth graders that numbered almost a thousand, from a wide range of socioeconomic backgrounds, all of us trying to find our place in this new world. Just walking the halls of West High those first few weeks was terrifying. In my insecurity, I needed a lifesaver to hold onto, and I found it.

At the end of the summer, after hours of practicing with my friends, we all tried out for the cheerleading squad, one of the few athletic opportunities for girls in 1961. One sophomore cheerleader and a sophomore alternate were selected each year. That sophomore cheerleader turned out to be me. This meant I would serve on the cheerleading squad for three years and become cheerleading captain in my senior year. It was my first salvation in high school—a place to channel enormous physical and emotional energy, a place to garner a small dose of affirmation, and a cheerleading uniform I could wear several days a week to compensate for a very small wardrobe.

I was wildly lucky when, at this pivotal point in my young adult life, I met two high school teachers who changed my life. They were very different from each other, but both knew how to empower an adolescent girl to reach down inside herself and pull out stars of accomplishment, achievement, and athleticism. They taught me to begin to value my body, my mind, and my spirit.

I met Carol Peterson, otherwise known as Pete, in tenth grade when she became my cheerleading coach and physical education teacher. She had short blond hair and was tan, freckled, and a great athlete. She could shoot a basketball, drive a golf ball, complete a great tennis serve, and do the butterfly in the swimming pool. She inspired us to reach for goals in sports we had never played before. We vied for singles, doubles, and team positions as we developed our rudimentary skills to compete against girls' teams from other schools.

This was long before Title IX, the 1972 federal law that prohibited sex discrimination in education and led to expanded access to sports for girls and women, among other things. Pete had organized a league with other women physical education teachers in the Minneapolis high schools. These women cared about girls having equal access to athletic opportunities, and they pursued this goal to the best of their ability with no funds or support from the school district. These fiercely passionate teachers were committed to giving girls every opportunity to learn to be team players, grow into team captains, and do their best on the field, the course, or the court, or in the pool. As we learned how to hold a tennis racquet, play defense on the basketball court, and discover the excitement of competitive indoor badminton, there was already a game scheduled or a meet time booked at the local pool. Little did we know how rare our opportunities were for girls at that time and what a gift these women were giving us.

We played our hearts out, working off new infusions of adolescent hormones, making skinny bodies muscular. Pete not only grew us into athletes, but also groomed us to be leaders. She ensured that we learned how to lose graciously and win humbly. All the while, she was committed to our winning recognition for our efforts, time, commitment, and passion.

In the course of becoming an athlete, I reckoned with my resentment that boys seemed to have it so easy, with lots of support for their teams. Students held sport rallies and pep fests for the boys. We held picnics for ourselves. It was just one more lesson on gender inequity.

At the end of the year, Pete held an awards picnic at her home for all the team participants. She surprised us that first year with large cloth athletic letters, just like the boys received for their letter jackets. Each year thereafter, we won brass medals for each sport to attach to our letters, just like the boys. With each year, we began to understand that we were breaking boundaries and making history in our own small way. I learned a power, strength, and confidence in my body I had not known before. I learned my body was something to take care of, condition, make strong, and value. My body was for me to use, not to be used by others.

That same year I met Charlotte Westby—Miss Westby, as students called her. She was West High's English teacher. I had seen her in the halls and found her to be intimidating and a bit scary. She had a 1940s hairstyle reminiscent of a Toni permanent. She wore eyeliner, rouge, and no lipstick. She rarely smiled and had an arm that, for a reason unknown to me, was limp; she held it down at her side as she walked the halls at a clipped, no-nonsense gait.

One day Miss Westby showed up at my tenth-grade homeroom and asked to speak to me. I didn't have her for a class, didn't know how she even knew who I was, and couldn't imagine why she wanted to talk with me. When I stepped into the hallway, she didn't introduce herself but informed me I would be the master of ceremonies for the National Honor Society program. I didn't know if I could do what she wanted, yet I was afraid to say no. She seemed to have made up her mind, so I acquiesced. I showed up for the first rehearsal and felt like a fish out of water. She walked me through the first rehearsals, barked at me through breaks, had me sing a solo and dance my way through the program. I did all of this in a court jester costume, which was also her idea.

At one point, I had to be honest with her, even though I was scared to do it. "Miss Westby, I need to ask you something." Because I hadn't asked for much, I had her attention. "Could you please not bark at me? You raise your voice and shout orders at me. I would do better if you could address me in a quieter way."

She looked at me with wide eyes, as if seeing me for the first time. "Of course. I didn't realize I was speaking loudly." With that exchange, we seemed to have a new relationship. I had never been on a stage before, but her coaching, guidance, and confidence in me made me rise to the occasion. We became an odd little team. Several more times, she tapped me to MC programs. Like many kids, I felt like an outsider in those years, even though other students may not have imagined it. Maybe Miss Westby and I were both outsiders in our own way, but her outsider believed in mine, banking on some unknown thread of possibility that she saw in me. From this vantage point in my life, I believe she saw the spirit in me.

It was my good fortune when she became my English teacher my senior year in high school. Together we wended our way through *Macbeth*, *The Canterbury Tales*, and *Tom Jones*. Through her teaching I became infatuated with poetry, fell in love with Shakespeare, learned to appreciate good literature, and plumbed my heart and soul searching for the deeper meaning of the printed word, iambic pentameter, and the melodic timbre of Old English and sonnets.

Sometimes Miss Westby invited me to stay after class and seemed genuinely interested to learn more about my mother, my family, and me. Most importantly, she listened. Knowing I came from a family in which no one had education beyond high school, she encouraged me to go to college. She cared about my heart—the heart she pulled out of the closet, put on stage, and inspired to pour out long-buried feelings, yearnings, and dreams in the papers I wrote for her. I don't know why she took this time and attention with me. But she did, and it changed my life.

If salvation can be found on a badminton court or on a stage, it was mine. If love can be embodied in a tan, athletic physical education teacher or a no-nonsense English teacher, that incarnation was there for me. If grace can be found in moving one's body or one's heart, that grace was mine, transforming a scared girl into a more confident young woman.

These two women, along with my mother, aunt, and grandmother, sent me into the world with righteous indignation and confidence, claiming my right to a place in the world beside men, ready to demand that I be taken seriously. If others wouldn't lead, then I would. It never occurred to me, after knowing these two women and living with the women in my family, that I wasn't equal. If men had a problem with that, it was their problem.

I was wildly lucky to have these women in my life begin to pull me out of a womb of shame and into those first steps of learning to love myself in all-new ways. I was born pure, shiny, and brand new. One man had stolen from me by invading my body and sexualizing me very young. His assaults left me terrified, tarnished, believing the world was a dangerous place. I felt compelled to protect my mother and myself by not exposing him, so the shame became mine to carry alone. Without knowing it, these two women walked with me on my journey to lay my burden down.

From my view as a woman in my seventies, I value this body that carried me to the bottom of the Grand Canyon just a few years ago. I value this heart that turns over in reading a lovely poem, this heart that is comforted by putting pen to paper, that seeks words for long-hidden experiences and untold stories. I value this spirit that carried me into the work where I was meant to be. It all began with these important women in my life.

## 20

# Vigil

## *1975*

My relationship with my mother was extraordinary, yet painfully complicated. Years of living with violence, fear, and anxiety took their toll on her health. These added layers of injury onto a heart already damaged by childhood rheumatic fever. I was left with relatives for extended periods of time when my mother was hospitalized for pneumonia and surgeries.

Growing up, I watched my mother's attempts to live a carefree life, to have male companionship, to feel loved. It all now makes sense, but back then I made more negative conclusions about men. I watched my mother date the wrong men: men who were married, old strange men, slick single men. In the balance sheet of experience, the legacy of instability, poor choices, and violence I had seen and experienced deepened my lack of trust.

As a child, I had an unusual need to keep order, accountability, and expectations for good behavior from my mother. At times we switched roles as parent and child. My mother would return from an evening out while I was home alone, waiting. As she came in the door, I'd stand with my hands on my hips and demand to know where she had been and why she was so late. And then there were the many trips to the emergency room, so her death always felt imminent. I always feared losing her.

At age forty-three, my mother required open-heart surgery to replace her damaged heart valves. In 1969 she entered a cardiac research program at Abbott Northwestern Hospital, which guaranteed all of her medical costs would be covered. The doctors told her that she might live seven more years after the surgery, but there were no guarantees. She was still willing to take the risk, so the doctors conducted experimental heart valve replacement using stainless-steel balls wrapped in Teflon-coated gauze. Those stainless-steel balls could be heard clicking against one another across the room. I used to tease her and ask her if it ever drove her crazy constantly hearing those balls clicking in her chest. She told me that it would bother her more if she didn't! During her hospitalization, she was in intensive care and could be visited only five minutes every hour. I decided to write her a letter to tell her what she meant to me.

In that letter, I tried to open the door to her past, my birth, and our violent history, but she wasn't willing to walk through. Weak though she was, with the help of a nurse, she wrote me a letter in return. "I chose to never marry because I didn't want a man to come into our lives and decide he was going to run your life. I wanted you to be free to determine your own life." This was her legacy to me as her daughter—that I could live to be free.

After weeks of recovery in the hospital, she moved in with me in my eighty-five-dollar-a-month apartment above the shops in a little neighborhood called Linden Hills. Soon a sixty-five-dollar-a-month studio apartment opened up down the hall, so I slapped a coat of paint on it and moved her. This helped her have some privacy and made it convenient for me to do her shopping and laundry while she recovered. I was a full-time student at the University of Minnesota and working three part-time jobs at the time, so I took out one student loan for tuition and another loan to pay our rents. As we had many times before, we survived.

After her heart surgery, my mother had a rebirth. It was the sixties. She moved into a commune with two other families, started an organic farm with like-minded folks, studied holistic medicine and reflexology, became a student of healthy eating and food supplements, joined the Unity Church, began work in the chemical dependency community, traveled by bus to faith healers, visited psychics, studied astrology, and started college for the first time in her life.

On New Year's Day, 1976, I was expecting her to arrive for dinner. Her friend Rose called. "Karla, your mother was supposed to come for lunch today. She never showed up. She never called. She's not answering her telephone." I hung up the telephone knowing I had lost her.

I didn't call anyone. I knew what I had to do. She and I had always gone it alone, and we would do this alone together as well. I got into my car and drove down the snowy streets of my neighborhood and then the freeway to St. Paul. Mom had moved to a nice studio in Kellogg Square Apartments near her job working for Human Development, a program that helped chemically dependent individuals find employment after treatment. She loved her job.

It was dark, and lights twinkled through the windows of homes where families gathered for a last holiday meal or to watch the bowl games. There weren't many cars on the snowy road, so I could travel slowly. I was in shock, devastated, frightened, but I had to hold it together for her. After arriving and parking in the lot for guests, I stopped at the security guard's office, told him I was concerned, and said I would call him if I needed help.

The door to my mother's apartment was locked, but for some reason she had not chained the door. She always chained the door. I entered her apartment, and it was dark. I could see her in the sofa bed, lying on her side, completely still. I was afraid. I sat down beside her, and she didn't move. I lifted the covers and could see the bottom half of her body was blue, like deep bruising. This made me even more scared. Had someone harmed her? (I learned later that if someone has been dead for a while, blood pools in the lower half of the body.) Then it really hit me. She was gone.

I leaned over and put my arm around her. "Oh, Mom! You can't leave me. Why didn't you listen to me?" My sorrow poured out of me, flowing onto her quiet body. I had never been in the presence of death before. It was peaceful, serene. I, the living, was the one in turmoil, in pain.

I sobbed until the stark reality hit me again with a new wave. I felt indignant. I got up and started to pace around her apartment, telling her how angry I was that she'd left me.

"I knew you were still sneaking cigarettes even with all your health talk. You had open-heart surgery, for God's sake. What were you think-ing? Didn't you care about me? It was so selfish of you. And then making all those crazy trips to Unity Village and faith healers, like you thought that would make a difference. Those people were just taking your money, playing on your fears. They were never going to cure you. Sometimes you launched your faith on the goofiest things. Your heart was broken. There was nothing they could do. There was nothing the doctors could do."

My rant left me exhausted, so I sat down in a chair in the dark and talked with her. "I can't believe you're leaving me alone. Not now, after all we've been through together. You're all I have. You're too young! I'm too young to lose you! I don't want to be alone. But we knew you were living on borrowed time. I know you tried so hard for both of us. I love you so much. I should've told you more. I should've spent more time with you."

I sat with her a while, holding the feeling of the two of us a little longer, knowing I would have to let her go, I would have to be the adult, I would take care of her as I had many times before.

Finally, I felt ready. I called the security office and asked the guard to do whatever he needed to do. Then I returned to her bed, sat down, and took the rollers out of her hair. I knew she would want to look nice for whoever came to help us.

It wasn't long before I heard a soft knock on the door. When I opened it, a young police officer was standing there. I told him, "My mother is dead, and I don't know what I'm supposed to do." He introduced himself, awkwardly expressed his sympathy, entered the room, and looked around. He suggested that my mother had likely gone to bed the night before and died in her sleep. "The position of her body is at rest. This tells me that she had no awareness of what was happening to her. Her heart probably just stopped. I need to call the coroner to come for her. This is procedure." I took some comfort in what he said.

I sat with my mother while he called the coroner's office. Then he returned, and we sat together while we waited. He told me he had never been called to a death or sat with a dead body in a home before.

"Isn't this a part of your training?" I asked him.

"Well, yes, but I'm pretty new in my job."

This was why he had drawn holiday duty. I felt I should offer him support.

"How old are you?" I asked.

"Twenty-six."

"Do they give you training on how to respond in these kinds of situations?"

"Yeah, sort of."

My heart went out to him. He seemed a bit uncomfortable. Meanwhile, my mother was there in her bed, a quiet presence in this strange moment.

"What am I supposed to do next?" I wondered out loud.

"We'll need the name of a funeral home from you, so the coroner knows who will pick up the body."

"I don't know any funeral homes!" I felt a bit panicked.

"Well, my father works in a funeral home, but it would be unethical of me to give you his name. Is there anyone you can call?" It hadn't occurred to me to call anyone, since I was so used to doing everything all alone. Then I remembered my mother's friend Carol. I called her, and she gave me the name of Enga Memorial Chapel.

Another soft knock. The police officer answered the door, and a young man came in wheeling a cart. This was the coroner's intern, who had also drawn holiday duty. After he gathered facts from the police officer and me, he sat down.

"How old are you?" I asked.

"Twenty-two." I was twenty-nine years old, and it occurred to me that I was the oldest individual dealing with this awful situation. I asked them if they were okay. The three of us talked over their discomfort and their individual need to have more experiences like this.

I asked them if they got training on grief. Not much, it turned out.

All the while, my mother sat vigil with us, and I suspected she was enjoying the course the conversation had taken. The three of us walked through the night together, muddling our way along, helping each other along the way.

Carol arrived with Reverend Jay Olson from Hennepin Avenue United Methodist Church. I had met him through a small group there, and Carol thought he might be able to help. It was time to remove my mother's body, so we stepped out of the apartment into the hall as the police officer assisted the coroner in moving my mother from her bed to the cart. When the door opened, my mother was on the cart covered in a white cloth. I realized this would be the last time I'd see her. I lay over her chest and held her for a moment. As the coroner wheeled her down the hall and onto the elevator, I felt the worst despair I had ever known. My mother was a deep part of me, and I was a deep part of her. Now she was truly gone. There was nothing to do but go home.

I woke early the next morning to discover many inches of light snow had fallen during the night, coating the world in lacy white detail. Though I had slept little, I was filled with restless energy and needed fresh air, so I plowed out into the deep snow, seeking solace on my walk. The world looked completely different. I realized the plates of my world had completely shifted in one night. I was filled with a profound grief, yet with each step into this natural beauty, a deep peace came over me.

On that walk, I felt an unexplainable spiritual shift take place. My suffering cut into my soul like never before. I felt the deepest grief and the most profound peace I had ever known, as if a presence were watching over me.

That day I made calls to my grandparents, aunts, and uncles and my mom's closest friends. I called Willie to let him know. We had been together off and on for several years. He returned my call from a phone booth in Wisconsin, and we cried together over the phone, his tears freezing to his face as he stood next to a country highway. He loved my mother. And she loved him—she'd told me, "If you don't marry Willie, I will!" He was heartbroken to hear this news.

I knew nothing about planning a memorial service, but Jay and Carol helped me. A memorial service was held in the small chapel at Hennepin Methodist, attended by my family, several friends, and my first husband and his mother. We had been divorced for seven years, but their thoughtfulness and concern for me were overwhelming. Their kindness didn't end with the service but continued with calls and staying in touch over several months. Mike and I had a couple dinners together and this provided the opportunity to express our regret over our individual immaturity when we married. We confirmed we had made the right decision to end our marriage.

In loss, we discover the generosity of spirit in others. Knowing I would have a lot of expenses, two male friends deposited money into my bank account without my knowledge. (The bank called me to let me know.)

Earle DeLaittre, whom I met through my work at the Science Museum of Minnesota, offered his home in Lowry Hill for a small reception. Two friends, Mike and Renee, made meals. Willie grieved with me and helped with legal questions.

A few weeks later, I received a call from Enga Memorial Chapel that my mother's ashes were ready. I drove alone—another one of those moments when it seemed right to be just the two of us. This was the first of several experiences of my mother's spirit still moving in and around me. When I arrived at the Enga Chapel, I met the funeral director and learned his son was the police officer I had met the day I found my mother. Through some mystery the officer's father had been the one to assist with her cremation. I wasn't surprised that her spirit was continuing to make connections happen. It was so like her.

The funeral director placed her in my arms as I had once been placed in her arms. I carried her to the car, sat her in the passenger seat in the black plastic box, and talked to her as I drove her home. I told her about my spiritual awakening on that snowy morning. I knew she would like that. Even with my spiritual epiphany, deep grief cracked me wide open, leaving me feeling wounded.

I went back to work, but I only communicated with a couple of friends. I sank into a deep depression that got even darker when my eleven-year-old dog had to be put to sleep. She had gone blind from glaucoma a couple years earlier, and her anxiety was making her crazy. She was suffering more than I was. She had been like my child for years and, recently, my comfort through months of grief and solitude. With the loss of my beloved dog, something shifted. It was as if a switch flipped and death began to feel more comfortable to me than life. I understood suicide for the first time. That was when a friend called and urged me to go to Chrysalis, a women's center, to get support.

In the ensuing months, I discovered that loved ones can visit you after they are gone. At first it was frightening. I came home from work one day and had the feeling someone was in my apartment. I walked through the kitchen, checked the dining room and then my bedroom. I gingerly entered the living room, and there was my mother, standing quietly in the corner, just being present, not speaking. It felt as if she were looking in on me, checking to see if I was okay. Thereafter, her appearances were softer, more as if she were resting on my shoulder, seeing the same scene I was, trying to tell me she was sorry I had to go through all of this because of her. On a clear, calm, sunny day, as I sat in a bank in downtown St. Paul, closing her bank accounts, I looked out the window and watched one lone tree flailing and thrashing as if being blown by a hurricane. I knew it was my mother expressing her regret that I had to do this alone.

In those months I practiced my own understanding of eternal life as I sprinkled some of her ashes in the garden behind my home on Irving Avenue. I scattered some of her ashes on my grandparents' farm. And I put some of her ashes in a pot containing a schefflera plant. My mother had rescued it after someone put it by the garbage chute. It was one stem with three tiny leaves. Over thirty years, that schefflera plant grew into a tree that climbed along the dining room ceiling in our home and shaded many family gatherings, celebrations with friends, and meaningful conversations. I liked to think my mother was eavesdropping, delighting in the fact that Willie and I were married, that we had two beautiful children, and that she got to share in it all. The plant thrived and grew so large it needed to be repotted by Bachman's nursery several times. "She lives" is real in a garden, on the farm, and in a flowerpot. Today I live down the street from the garden where her ashes enrich the soil and encourage flowers. I give her a nod as I walk my grandson and my dogs through the neighborhood. Now she knows I'm okay.

# 21

## Mining Truths

### *1978*

I stood looking at the doorknob. I could feel my entire body shaking. I was one second away from walking back to my car and going home. I knew if I turned the knob and opened the door, it would be a statement to those inside the room that I had lived through the same hell they had. No one was more surprised than I to be standing there.

A couple of months earlier, on a beautifully snowy day, my friend Luise and I had taken the bus downtown to see a movie. Afterward, we had adjourned for dinner to Ichabod's, a popular bar on Seventh Street. I hadn't known Luise long, but we were fast becoming good friends. She was the executive director at Chrysalis, where we met. I had entered the facilitator training program, and when it ended, she had contacted me to see if I would co-facilitate a women's group on depression.

We nestled into a table at the bar, ordered our dinner, and settled in for some good conversation. Luise was an insightful woman who asked good questions with sensitivity. As two women getting to know each other, we gradually peeled back the layers. We had each lost a parent within the last year, and those losses were a shared experience most of our friends did not grasp.

As we talked, I began letting down my guard and sharing more about my chaotic childhood and life in Texas, when my mother and I lived with Gene. Luise continued to ask questions, seeming to grasp that there was more to my story. I had never really spoken in detail with anyone about those years, but Luise seemed empathetic when she asked me to be more specific. In that dark bar, we donned our headlamps and wended our way down into a mine filled with buried memories.

Maybe it was being in this warm, intimate cocoon of a bar, which had been blanketed by fresh-fallen snow, or maybe it was the tenderness of a kind woman friend, but in that moment, I felt safe enough to share my memories about what happened to me as a little girl. I brought those nuggets forth into the lamplight and laid them on the table. She didn't do what I feared most—act disgusted. She didn't minimize what I had told her. She didn't laugh at the impossibility of such things happening to a child. She simply sat there and listened and showed me her sadness over what had happened to me. It was a profound experience of being heard.

When I had said all that was within my power to remember, I was exhausted. We sat there, letting the words fall and settle softly like the snowflakes outside the window. The words didn't drift but landed in banks of hard truth between us. We let them sit there for a while, and then she leaned in, looked me right in the eye, and said, "This is going to be very hard to hear, but I need to say it anyway. You are a victim of incest." I couldn't believe what I heard. I wanted to deny the ugly words she had said.

"But this man wasn't my father."

"It doesn't matter. You lived with him in a relationship as if he were your father. There was no difference. What he did to you was the same as incest, as if you were his own child. The impact on you emotionally, psychologically, and physically is the same."

Her words took my breath away, and all I could do was weep.

We continued to talk about years of trust issues, problems establishing intimate relationships, and my inability to make commitments. We talked about what I had been living with for years: loss, pain, anger, fear, and, most importantly, shame—the deep feeling of being flawed.

So here I was, months later, standing in the Ramsey County Public Health Building outside a room where an incest support group was meeting. If I opened the door, every person in that room would know why I was there. Fear and shame gripped me as I held that doorknob, unable to turn the handle. My deepest yearning was to feel whole and well. I was working through layers of discovery after my mother's death, first learning who my birth father was and now this. It felt as if there were no end—but I wanted the pain and shame to end. I sucked up all the courage I had, turned the doorknob, and entered the room.

As I walked in, I went down into the mine, carrying my own lamp. Just ask anyone who has suffered abuse of any form. It is descending deep into unfathomable darkness. Over many years, I have tunneled through the realities of my childhood with the aid of professional helpers using sticks of dynamite, jackhammers, and pickaxes to dislodge the accumulated losses caused by emotional and spiritual damage. The remaining debris blocked an inability to feel spiritual wholeness and essential goodness. Over even more years, it has taken fine dental tools to pick through the remaining memories to reclaim those feelings.

# 22

# Lessons in Trust

I began seminary in 1988, a four-year journey into learning about scripture, Christian history, systematic theology, and ethics. Yet I was yearning for something more. I felt the need to take all of this education into my heart and learn to pray. Where better to learn to pray than from my Catholic sisters? So I applied to enter spiritual direction training at Sacred Ground at the Carondelet Center in St. Paul. We were required to have our own spiritual director during the process.

Helen was my spiritual director for almost a year. One day she looked at me with her kind eyes and asked, "Can you be as compassionate with yourself as God is with you?"

I moved back on my blue-upholstered wingback chair and took what felt like the first really deep breath I had taken in years. It had been such hard work trying to heal, trying to replace the essential missing piece of myself taken by Gene. I had spent years being driven, judging myself, being hard on myself, not forgiving myself. I breathed in this new idea and exhaled memories of working so hard to make it feel better. Maybe living didn't have to be such hard work after all.

"I've never felt compassion for me," I said. "I've mostly been ashamed of me. To overcome those feelings, my response was to be strong, confrontational, come out swinging—with words or, as a little girl, by sticking my tongue out at leering construction workers. In eighth grade I stabbed a kid with a lead pencil for telling me my breasts looked like the photos of the Greek statues in our art room. No one was going to take anything away from me or my body again without me putting up a battle."

I spoke with intensity, and my breath came faster as I tried to explain why it had been so hard.

After listening to my rant, Helen said again, "I'm simply asking you if you can be as compassionate with yourself as God is with you." Memories of my efforts to heal what had been wounded rose to the surface. I knew that according to research, if a child has one caring adult in their life, their chance of survival is greatly increased. My mother and grandparents had been there for me. Two high school teachers had been there for me. I established a foundation for trust early in my life through friendships, opening myself to feeling worthy to be loved, and learning I could survive risking love. Sitting in Helen's office, I began to recount those building blocks and how essential and important they were to me.

It began with friendships.

"Can you do 'skin the cat'?" My first invitation to be a friend came on the monkey bars in third grade. I had arrived in Minneapolis with my grandparents' love in my back pocket, one year of first grade in a one-room country schoolhouse in my backpack, and my mother's promise in my heart. It was my first day in a city school. A blond girl flipped off the question to me as she slid her belly over the edge of the monkey bars, reached under and across, grabbing the opposite bar, and then swung her whole body over the edge and swung back and forth, holding on tight. I hadn't known how to skin the cat before, but now I had an idea.

"Sure, I can." I fumbled my way through my first try.

"That's how you do it." Her praise caught me as I swung there myself, dangling in midair, holding on for dear life. That's how the little blond girl, Patsy, and I connected.

When my mother moved us to Albert Lea for one year, it was hard, but when I returned, Patsy and I became inseparable. Like sisters, we had each other's backs, but we competed with each other over sports and school activities. We argued about who had life tougher. Patsy's mother, Pauline, was a widow by the time Patsy was a year old, and they were on Aid for Families with Dependent Children, otherwise known as welfare. My mother was divorced and worked at a couple different jobs, which bore its own embarrassment. Compared to other kids at school who had moms and dads and lived in nice houses, we both felt different, so we bonded as outsiders.

By seventh grade, Patsy and I got to know Kay. She was from a family of five kids, with a sweet mother and an alcoholic father. Through Kay I discovered that other kids had wounds in themselves, too, but for different reasons from mine. Patsy, Kay, and I struck out into the world with an important common shared experience: absent fathers. We navigated friendship and boy crushes, and we shared our deepest secrets when we had sleepovers. Michele became a member of our little band of friends after she joined the cheerleading squad in high school. But as close as we were, I never shared my darkest secret. Still, these friendships have sustained me for over sixty-five years.

Even in those years, I raised my antenna ten feet high around boys and men, ever vigilant and watchful. I watched Kay's father carefully when I was at her house. He reminded me of Gene: his anger sucked all the oxygen out of their very large home, and the children scattered. I was sensitive to any hint of danger. I got angry at any sign of disrespect from men, especially if I thought I wasn't being taken seriously.

Then it happened, in my sophomore year in high school: my first serious relationship with a boy. To other kids it might have looked like a "boy meets girl, they like each other, and they start dating" scenario. With my history, it meant daring to risk being close to a male person. All my fight-or-flight instincts were on high alert. I knew very little about male human beings other than they were not to be trusted. Up to this point, my grandfather was the only man in my young life I could trust. It took time, but very slowly I sensed this boy's kind spirit. He showed respect for me, and, eventually, I let him come close. He was considerate, kind, thoughtful, and made me feel valued and respected.

As we got to know one another, I suffered fear, insecurity, and bouts of inadequacy, yet he patiently rode those tumultuous tides with me. I had no understanding of the hidden hot currents of shame that governed my lack of well-being and self-worth. He was patient with my unexpected responses and reactions based on life experiences beyond what any sixteen-year-old boy could be expected to understand. At one point, this curly-haired, brown-eyed, ruddy-cheeked boy asked me to be his girl, and I said yes.

To our parents and other adults, we were an unlikely pair. Compared to his affluent family and their life of private clubs and corporate executive neighbors, my low-income family life and single mother were not what they expected for their son. While we ate on TV trays at my house, his parents' dinner table held forks with more assignments than I knew existed. His lovely, kind mother coached me on the silverware in the candlelight, while his dignified bank president father dished up everyone's dinner plate from the head of the table. None of this mattered to the dear boy. It was a huge gift to a girl who sang alone in the bathtub in scary times and watched her family go through a murder trial, but none of my past could be brought into the candlelight and served up on fine china at the dinner table. It remained a secret.

After graduation, when the young man left for Yale, he wrote his heart on pages in letters as I suffered back home in my senior year of high school. During one fall visit to see him at Yale, something clicked. Our class differences stared me in the face as we walked along ivy-draped walkways, as I tried to fit in among girls from eastern colleges who wore pearls and expensive clothes, as I stood in the sea of confidence and entitlement that surrounded him. I couldn't swim in those waters. Even though that wasn't who he was, I was drowning in shame and insecurity. I returned home, waiting for my menstrual cycle, and got scared. My greatest fear was that I would get pregnant and be an embarrassment to him and his family. I was forced to make a hard decision. I didn't want to make a mistake I would regret for the rest of my life. I returned to Minnesota knowing the relationship would end. In our five years together, though, I learned about trust. He had set the bar high for any future relationships. Thereafter, I only chose kind men like him.

As I tried to move forward, I felt muddled up inside. When my aunt used a shotgun to end her pain, I learned down deep that sometimes a woman had to hurt so as not to get hurt. I learned that sometimes a woman had to risk disappearing inside prison, on a Greyhound bus, or inside her own soul to save herself when situations got too frightening. These early lessons did not foster my ability to create lasting, trusting relationships.

Sadly, I bewildered a lot of very kind men over the years as I tried to understand myself. Due to a breast cancer scare, I dropped out of college. At the same time, my mother filed bankruptcy. Then I met the man who became my first husband. He was kind, thoughtful, and responsible, and had charted a course for himself to be a civil engineer. He had a wonderful family and presented me with stability and security as I had never known them before. I believed I loved him, and I leaped, trying to trust him and myself, but I was unprepared for marriage. I had vowed to myself that I would never divorce, but it wasn't long before I knew I could not remain married. To say I felt like a failure minimizes the impact of that decision on me.

Now I not only carried my old fears, but added a new fear of failing in another marriage. I remember looking around and thinking that others seemed to navigate relationships so easily, but not me. What did they know that I didn't know? My journey to understanding the underlying causes of my fear had not yet begun.

Then I met the kindest man of all, the man who is now my husband.

Men who end up in relationships with women from abusive backgrounds need enormous patience. Even though I loved Willie dearly, I was stuck in fear: fear of intimacy, fear of failure in another marriage, fear that this man would hurt me or leave me. For thirteen years we were on and off again as Willie patiently waited for me to get clarity, to become more trusting. During those years I sought psychological and emotional help in small steps. Whether we were on or off in our relationship, we consistently celebrated important holidays with our mothers, attended the opera, and did all of our significant traveling together. No matter who each of us might otherwise be dating, they had to accept the arrangement as it was.

At long last, Willie threw down the gauntlet and said we needed to decide whether to marry, so we entered premarital counseling. Even with the help of a good therapist, I was still frozen in fear and could not make the commitment. Willie said he was done. He wanted a family, and we were approaching our mid-thirties. We stopped seeing each other.

For several months I grieved the loss of the relationship and contemplated moving to take a job in California. It would be an easy escape, but the thought of leaving Willie behind broke my heart. Yet I was still terrified. One day, unexpectedly, Walt Pulliam, the minister at Judson Church, called and invited me to lunch.

During the meal, Walt looked at me with his kind blue eyes and said, "I want to hear all about the job in California, but first, what's going on with Willie?" Walt had learned about our breakup through a mutual friend. I burst into tears and poured out all my fears, regrets, and grief. He listened intently and then said quietly, "That job in California sounds amazing, but I suspect you first need to resolve this grief over Willie."

In that moment I felt peace. I can't explain it. Learning to trust is hard work. I had been struggling hard to understand my fear, but something released, and I felt a crossing-over experience that was deeply spiritual. Calm came over me, and I knew what I needed to do. After lunch I went straight to the Science Museum's gift shop, bought a ring with dinosaurs on it, called Willie, and invited him to take a walk. On a bench by Lake of the Isles, I proposed. He was stunned. "Are you sure you aren't going to change your mind?" He was so surprised that he asked me this question several times. It was understandable after all we had been through together.

"I am absolutely sure." It was as if the plates of my very being had shifted, moved into the place they were meant to be, and settled. I ordered flowers to be delivered to his office the next day with a card that read, "I still haven't changed my mind."

Four months later we were married by Walt before two hundred of our friends and colleagues. After our thirteen-year relationship, they wouldn't have believed we got married unless they witnessed it themselves. Forty years of marriage later, the power of abuse still rears its ugly head, but its impact has been greatly diminished over the years by the love and patience of Willie, my children, and dear friends. The little card from the flowers is now framed and stands on the bookshelf by my reading chair, a gift to Willie on a wedding anniversary. And I still haven't changed my mind.

# 23

## Journey of the Spirit

When I was nine, I believed I met God on my bedroom wall in the form of my glow-in-the-dark Jesus. Still, God felt out of reach. At age fourteen, I tried to know God more intimately as I chose to be baptized and confirmed in the Presbyterian church, but mostly because my best friend was doing it. In my twenties, I was drawn to Hennepin Avenue United Methodist Church, where Chester Pennington was the pastor. I had attended grade school with his daughter, Celeste, and gone to slumber parties in the parsonage next door. I had fond memories of sliding down the marble staircase in our flannel pajamas. Boy, you could really fly!

It was the 1960s, and Hennepin Methodist had invited a Black congregation to merge with their church. Many of the wealthy white church members fled west to the suburbs. On the Sunday morning after Dr. Martin Luther King Jr. was assassinated, Dr. Pennington stood in the pulpit and said, "On this day, I want to come before you not only as your pastor, but as a man who is grieving. I want to invite Harry Davis, another man who is grieving, to join me." Davis was a community leader and member of the newly joined Black congregation. With those words, Dr. Pennington removed his clergy robe. These two men stood in the pulpit together as friends and shared their grief for our country. The image of these two men standing in the pulpit together and the substance of their words pierced my heart. They put personal words to what the nation was feeling.

On another Sunday, Mother's Day, Dr. Pennington said he felt there was someone more qualified to address women's concerns, so he stepped out of the pulpit and invited his seminary-educated wife to preach. Mrs. Pennington stood in the pulpit and, with conviction and clarity, said these words: "Every woman, child, and person of color in this country has the right to question the role of the white American male." I had never heard such words in church before.

Then, in 1974, I met two remarkable women, Lois and Elizabeth. The three of us worked together in the Education Department at the Science Museum of Minnesota. Lois worked with volunteers, and Elizabeth was the Native American teacher on the staff. We conceived, designed, and implemented programs for children, adults, volunteers, and museum members. Over lunch we talked about our projects, but more importantly, as we got to know each other more intimately, we talked about beliefs, doubts, and what was important to us. They had each grown up in a church and were active in their congregations, so at times we talked about our understandings of scripture. Since I had grown up unchurched, I valued these conversations. I was drawn to these two women because of their expansive hearts, their nonjudgmental manner, and their willingness to listen. They had seen me dive deep into depression in the months after my mother's death. They were concerned about me. They knew I was trying to make sense of all that was happening in my life, and I was doing it alone.

One day, in a quiet, unassuming way, Elizabeth asked me if I would like to attend a dinner at her church. It was a Seder hosted by a Jewish family for the congregation. It sounded intriguing, so I said yes. As I sat there in the fellowship hall of Judson Church, I looked around the room at the warm faces of friendly strangers and experienced the welcoming hospitality of the community. I felt as at home as I could feel in any church at that time in my life. There was an open and accepting spirit as the mother of the Jewish family stood up and said she and her husband had brought their children to the church to "hear the rest of the story."

Because of the life experiences I carried, I had always felt unacceptable in church. We seldom went to church when I was on the farm, but when I was around twelve years old, my grandmother took me to a Methodist country church one Sunday. I remember sitting next to my grandmother, listening to the pastor preaching about our sins and shame. I took in every word and was convinced he was talking about me. When he invited those who wanted to be forgiven and saved to come to the front of the church, I bolted out of my seat, raced past my grandmother, and found myself heading down the center aisle, sobbing. I didn't know what had come over me, but I wanted the shame to be gone and was willing to do anything to make it go away.

Later, I tried to enter church communities but stayed only briefly. Sitting at that Passover dinner, I thought this might be a place I could feel comfortable. They had welcomed the other stranger. Maybe they could also welcome me. I describe my entry into the church this way: my Native American friend and her Irish husband took me to a Jewish Passover Seder at the Baptist church.

I knew nothing then about Judson Church or American Baptists, but I learned over time that it was a progressive, social justice–minded community. The American Baptists split from the other Baptists over the issue of slavery, turning north instead of south. American Baptists have ordained women since the late 1800s. They have no creeds to recite, which appealed to me because I didn't want to recite words and statements of belief that I didn't understand. I learned this was part of the free church movement, which sought freedom from church leaders determining what others needed to state in order to belong.

The concept of "soul freedom," which I learned about over time, meant there was no intermediary—no priest or pastor—interpreting scripture. This was between God and me. That principle helped me feel at ease because no man was telling me what to believe. Baptists also dedicate babies and then baptize young adults when they choose to be baptized, a practice known as Baptism of the Believer. I had chosen my own baptism at age fourteen, so this made sense to me as well. As I sat in the embrace of stained glass windows and warm wood, I didn't know then that this church building was rather fancy for plain Baptists.

Despite my past reservations about getting involved in a church, I was drawn there every week. That beautiful space became a sanctuary for mourning. I entered the church each Sunday, sat in the back pew, and allowed my heart to be penetrated by the music and by Walt's words at the pulpit and I wept. The personal reflections shared by members of the congregation from a second pulpit had a profound impact on me. I had never imagined that such intimate feelings of doubt, disappointment, grief, joy, blessing, or gratitude could be shared in church by ordinary people. Listening, I didn't feel so alone.

Frequently I slipped out of church early so others wouldn't see my red, swollen eyes. In time, I lingered in the pew, and another church member, Dave Weaver, with his own eyes red and a hanky at his nose, would pat my shoulder as he walked down the center aisle, making us comrades in our tears. At one point he laughingly told me, "I call myself Leaky Dave!"

Over several years, something happened. Between the personal work I was doing and my experiences in a faith community, I took new risks that were life-changing. I had been stuck, paralyzed by fear and anxiety. Now I began to get clarity about how I wanted to live my life. Within five years I got married, bought a home, changed jobs twice, and adopted two babies. I was learning how to live freely. And then something deeper began to tug at my heart. The arrival of my children had everything to do with this newfound wonder. I didn't understand it or have words for it at the time, but I wanted to dive in and take it deeper.

Dorothy Day once said that in the moment her child was laid in her arms, there "came a desire to adore, to worship, and to serve, to pass along this gift." Each time one of my babies came off the airplane and was placed in my arms, the plates of my soul shifted. I experienced love as I could never imagine. I understood the depth of my mother's love for me in a completely new way. I began to reflect on my aunt Lila's actions and the love force behind her choices as I never had before.

I now lived in an intact, stable family of my own for the first time in my life. I once commented to my husband, "So this is what other kids had." As I watched my daughter and son play, I witnessed what a safe childhood was like as I gave them security and constancy day by day. It was the greatest joy I had ever known. Yet I also felt the deepest sorrow. I missed my mother as I had never missed her before. I unearthed my losses, layer by layer, and grieved deeply. I also felt that if I could love my children this deeply, and if there was some great goodness in the universe that was supposed to love me just as much or more, then I wanted to know more about that goodness.

At that point in my unchurched history, I didn't know the words of the prophet Jeremiah: "You shall find me when you shall search for me with all your heart" (29:13).

At every job I held, I saw how life issues and challenges were an integral part of what individuals brought with them to work every day. I found myself desiring more and more to be with people in those important places, in their living and their dying, rather than working on concerns of performance, compensation, and professional goals.

One year I enrolled in a nine-day executive development program at the Carlson School of Management. At the end of the program, participants were supposed to state what they had gleaned from the experience. Knowing I was going to be out of step, I stated that I had figured out I didn't really care about the bottom line. I was going to seminary.

That yearning took me to United Theological Seminary for my first interview with Karen Smith Sellars, the director of admissions. I told her I didn't know what I believed about God, and that Jesus was still a mystery to me, but I wanted to enter seminary. She asked me if I'd had a "road to Damascus experience." My reply was "What is that?" To her credit, she still welcomed me in as a new student.

My seminary education began a journey toward healing I could not have imagined. It helped me learn a new language for my life experiences as I studied process theology with Mary Bednarowski and Don White. I learned that my questions were encouraged.

I learned from Henry Gustafson that it was okay to be reading scripture for the first time in my life in my early forties—"better now than later," he said as he smiled kindly at me. Writing systematic theology papers for Mary Potter Engel, I received affirmation as I wrote from my life experience. It was a revelation to me that my faith understanding began with the experience of evil as I struggled to write an ethics credo for Jim Nelson. His admiration for my soul-searching work gave me strength.

I came to understand more deeply that if a child is invaded and thrust into being a sexual person, the power of that secret and experience becomes the lens through which the world and all relationships are viewed, the lens through which all physical contact is experienced, the lens through which feeling loved by God or not is determined. I needed deep taking-apart and reconstruction. It took me straight to therapy.

The first time I sat in Dick Jones's office, I told him, "I want to come here, feel safe enough to cry so hard I can have snot dripping off my chin, and not need to look good. I need a male therapist who can handle whatever comes up because I may take it out on you." He suggested three initial visits, which turned into more than two years of sessions. Lowering myself down into the secrets took time.

Dick's professional skill, wisdom, sensitivity, honesty, and compassion enabled me to dig deep into the mines of my childhood. He was acutely aware of my hypervigilance and need to feel safe, so each time I arrived or left his office, he put his hands in his pockets so he wouldn't touch me by mistake. He was tuned into my fears, kept strict boundaries, and showed me respect.

When I first spoke of myself as a little girl, I found myself rejecting her, feeling disdain for her. I was embarrassed by her, ashamed of her. I was the adult woman trying to keep that little girl locked and barred outside the door of Dick's office. She did nothing but cause me trouble. I wanted nothing to do with her. I was that separated from myself, that lacking in integration of self. One man had the power to cause a little girl to feel so ugly, with so little value, that she couldn't feel any compassion for herself.

At one point in my sessions, Dick asked me if I had a photograph of Gene. I knew there were photos of him in one of my mother's old albums in a cardboard box in storage. He suggested I bring the photos in to see if they would help me dislodge frozen memories and feelings. That week I approached the storeroom in my basement. The old demons rustled around me from every direction. I spotted the cardboard box in the corner. The dark power of that box radiated off the shelf, making it difficult to pick up. Before my next appointment I placed the box in the passenger seat of my car. Knowing Gene's photo was in that box felt as if he were in the car beside me. My mouth was dry and I was sweating when I arrived at Dick's office. When he asked me if I wanted to open the box, I was adamantly against it. "That's okay. I'll put it in the closet, and when you're ready, we'll take it out." The box remained in his closet for over a year.

In all that time, all I could do was mourn my losses as a little girl. At times it seemed I arrived in Dick's office to simply have a safe place to sit and weep. Now that I had my own children, I saw their purity and innocence. I watched their delight in their own bodies, how they loved to run around the house after their baths, naked, laughing, being silly, and feeling so safe. There was no shame. I more deeply understood all that Gene had stolen from me: my innocence, my value for myself, my body, my ability to trust, to attach, to have faith in men, to feel safe and secure. In addition to the renewed grief I felt for my mother, I felt profound sorrow for that little girl I had barred outside the door.

The day came when Dick suggested it might be time to look at the photographs. With my heart pounding and great trepidation, I agreed. I had to be brave and take back the power and control this man had over my life, even as a grown woman. I felt nauseated and shaky as I opened the box and examined the photos of Gene, my mother, and me. In every photograph, Gene smiled confidently while there was no joy or light behind my mother's eyes. I was still frozen. The photos jarred nothing loose. I could not get enraged on my own behalf over what this man had taken from me. It wasn't until I tried hypnosis, at Dick's suggestion, that the rage welled up.

Seminary provided my second crossing-over experience. I didn't have as much baggage to unpack as many of my classmates who arrived from more conservative backgrounds. Patient, thoughtful, kind professors companioned me on my unorthodox journey into my own theological understandings. I had to do the work in my own way, and it didn't fit the typical path.

Willie and my children, Kate and Zack, attended my seminary graduation wearing T-shirts that said "Mom's Cheerleaders." Then it was on to the ordination process. In our denomination, the first step was writing an ordination paper stating my theology on traditional Christian doctrines such as God, Jesus, eschatology, sin, grace, and so on. I was then required to present my paper in person to the denominational church ministry committee and answer their questions.

Few women were being ordained in American Baptist churches, and the ordination process wasn't easy. I had written my ordination paper theologically reflecting on my own life experience rather than repeating standard doctrinal answers. As one woman said, "Your ordination paper is beautiful, but it doesn't fit the template. If you can explain it to me, that would be helpful." Fortunately, Stan Borden, a lifelong American Baptist and respected member of the committee, looked each of his fellow members right in the eye and said, "This is one of the clearest and most beautifully written papers I have ever read. Karla is well suited to ministry." I could have kissed him for being so kind, understanding, and generous. Making it through the hoops of the church as a woman in the 1980s was no small matter.

Once approved by the Church Ministry Committee for ordination, every candidate was required to go before an ordination council, which was a gathering of representatives from all the Twin Cities area churches. On the day of my meeting with the ordination council, I was feeling nervous and rose at 5:30 a.m. When I walked into the front sunroom of my home, standing on my lawn in the middle of the city were three deer. I anointed them the triune deer and knew everything would be okay. I told the ordination council about the deer, and it set the tone for what turned out to be an affirming and generous experience.

On the day of my ordination, Lois and Elizabeth both spoke from the pulpit, along with Rev. Dale Edmondson; Walt; Al Baez, a dear Quaker friend; and my invited guests. They had all set me on the path for this journey. I wanted to honor and thank them in any way I could.

I had no idea that more grace awaited me in cemeteries and funeral chapels. Following three years of working in the church, I took a position with Community Chaplain Services through TRUST (Toward Renewed Unity in Service Together) member churches in South Minneapolis. It was a bereavement and funeral ministry for individuals and families outside the church. In four years, I officiated 350 funerals or memorial services for families from different cultural, socioeconomic, and faith backgrounds. Someone in a family had died, something needed to happen, and families didn't know what to do, so I helped them create a service of remembrance. These families dealt with suicides, murders, infant losses, sudden deaths, and deaths from long-term illnesses. It was my own small kindness to strangers.

Estrangement was a recurring theme in these families. They were estranged from the church due to hurt, anger, rigid rules, or just never connecting. They were estranged from one another for the same reasons.

I learned the importance of forgiveness from these families' stories. Together we waded through their losses. From the first phone call to my wave goodbye at the cemetery, they showed me the enduring raw grief that comes with estrangement and death. Again, I learned I wasn't alone.

As I watched wailing family members caress caskets and lay their bodies over hard wood in one last embrace, my heart broke. I lost any hesitation to forgive, to release any last vestiges of resentment toward my mother or any unloved places within myself. I kneaded my own grief, and out of that pain rose an ability to companion others as they loved their dear ones through illness to their death. Many of these families had lived hard lives that included alcohol, drugs, and multiple divorces, experiences not unlike my own family. These were my people. As I ministered to them, they ministered to me.

Following four years in bereavement and funeral ministry, I rested and waited to discern what I was meant to do next. A colleague called and encouraged me to return to hospital ministry, since I had loved my post-seminary internship at Ramsey Medical Center. I applied to three hospitals and was accepted at all three. I chose North Memorial because of the communities it served, and I was anxious to learn from Janet Labrecque, a respected and skillful clinical pastoral education supervisor. I entered chaplaincy at age fifty-five and found the place I was always meant to be. Guided by Janet's wisdom, my colleagues in residency, Patty, Jody, and Pam, and I waded into deep waters, both in patient care and within ourselves.

We learned that if we were going to be with others where they lived and where they died, we needed to be unafraid to feel pain and hurt alongside them with deep compassion, risking our own hearts in the process. In my fourteen years as a hospital chaplain, I met many intact, faithful families and individuals, but I also continued to meet my people: individuals and families who knew estrangement or felt they were outside the door of the church, who needed to feel loved and accepted wherever they were, not where the church expected them to be.

I met patients in the thin places in their lives where questions about life and death were on their hearts. I remember the gentleman on hospice who told me he felt the presence of Jesus in his room. "I felt him. He went *whoosh* right over my shoulder to let me know he was here."

Ruby greeted me with, "Where have you been? I've been waiting for you all day. I have a question for you."

"What's on your mind?" She had piqued my curiosity.

"Well, I understand we see our loved ones after we die. How do I make sure I see husband number one and not husband number two?"

Because of my previous visits with Ruby, I knew she had a good sense of humor and that she might be teasing me.

"Imagine the problem Elizabeth Taylor has!" We had a good laugh together, which is also good medicine.

I recall the day I was paged to the intensive care unit to meet with a patient. Her immediate words to me were, "Help me help my children let me die." Working in a Level I trauma center, we chaplains witnessed tragedies and dramas we would never have imagined, but it was often in those quiet moments when profound exchanges happened, when beliefs were less important than keeping faith with one another, maintaining a presence when others left. Every day I learned about courage and strength from these individuals and families and the staff with whom I worked.

Soon after I began my chaplaincy, I realized the need for care and support of the staff in the hospital. Along with my colleague Sue Brost in the Employee Health Clinic and Mark Berg, one of the hospital doctors, we proposed the LifeWork Program for employees. In the first year, it had over one thousand points of contact as employees reached out for support through one-to-one contacts, small groups, or special programs geared to their needs. Employees entrusted me with their family struggles, secrets, losses, and employment challenges.

We offered "Compassionate Conversations" in the chapel over the noon hour, which I co-facilitated while employees shared their experiences with particular life transitions, focusing on how they coped and how they found meaning in the experience. Employees attended conversations on more than forty different topics, including infant death, surviving sexual assault, parenting adult children, losing a spouse, and living with a diagnosis. The combination of patient and staff care was the most gratifying experience in my fifty years of working.

However, no matter how much I grew over those years, there was still room for more internal housecleaning and renovating. One day I ran into Patricia Hoolihan, who had been my writing instructor in a memoir class. We stood outside a pharmacy and talked about the classes she was teaching at the Loft Literary Center, a local organization that offers writing classes and other programs for writers. She said she was interested in teaching a new class called "Writing as a Tool for Healing." She was searching for a venue, so I told her I'd try to come up with a place.

The next day, I called her and proposed that she hold the class at my house. Within weeks, eight women were gathered around my dining room table, writing for the purpose of healing. In time, we christened the class Karla's Table.

One of the early pieces I wrote and read in the class was a chapter of my aunt Lila's story. It was very hard to read. My heart pounded, my mouth was dry, my voice quavered—all old familiar symptoms of shame. At that time in my life, I wondered what the women in the class would think of me and how they would respond to this sordid family story. Some were neighbors or people I knew from my community. My old outsider identity kicked in. I feared their judgment. I did not yet know their stories, so I had not discovered the pain or losses they might bring to the class. But they could not have been more compassionate, encouraging, and loving in their support.

For eight years we have gathered at the table together, shared the communion of our writing, loved and held one another as we've taken turns reading powerful stories with raggedy breath and tears, knowing our stories would land on a table set with love and compassion. In the context of this care, additional stories rose to the surface, and each piece of writing took me toward more healing. To write the stories involved a deeper reconciliation with my past, my mother, and my family. To journey into the past, the trauma, and the experiences in my family required resolve, support, and faith. The women in the class gave me all of that and more. I've also drawn inspiration from Etty Hillesum in her book *An Interrupted Life*. She wrote, "If God cannot help me, then I shall have to help God."

Through my faith, even when I haven't had words for it, I've been writing my way to freedom. Today I feel free to write, paint, dance, create, love. I have been writing this story in my heart for fifty-five years. But now I have put words, sentences, verbs, paragraphs together to give secrets shape and form. I have written these stories as a tribute to my mother and my aunt, as well as other women, so they know they are not alone. I have written this story for me. No more secrets. Only freedom.

When I turned the doorknob to the room where the incest support group was meeting, I had rolled the last stone away from the tomb of isolation I had been living within. I conceded I was willing to be vulnerable, to be honest with myself and, eventually, with others about the truth of my life experience. Little did I know it would include my family, beloved friends, a faith community, a therapist, a seminary faculty, dear colleagues, writing companions, and total strangers. Anyone who has had these experiences, whose life story includes stolen childhood innocence and undergoing domestic violence, will understand.

Frederick Buechner wrote, "Theology is, at its heart, autobiographical." In the middle of my life something snapped. It was not the crack of a twig, but rather a huge branch wrenching itself loose from the frozen tree of me. The branch fell, taking with it fear, anxiety, doubts, and secrets. As it crashed to the earth, it left me wrenched loose, lighter, able to lift my head, heart, and spirit. Slowly, I began to move, reach, bend, leap. I had been frozen for sixty years, but now I could see the rings of my life more clearly. I could add more rings. I took off my pinstriped suit, stepped out of the boardroom, and drove to the seminary. I wasn't sure what I was looking for, but I was sure it would find me, and it did.

That frozen tree was now bending with the weight of love, babies, a home, church, community, and the Spirit. Live sap began to flow, buds turned green and leafed out. The overstory of the tree of me became lush and full, able to provide protection for my family and shade for my grandchildren. Today I am at peace in my small forest of family.

# 24

## The Rocking Chair

### *2014*

I sit in my living room, holding my two-week-old grandson, Liam, in an antique rocking chair. This dark oak rocker, with rich blue upholstery emblazoned with red, cream, gold, orange, and sky-blue diamond-shaped patterns, has held many babies, including my own children, Kate and Zack, in more than a hundred years of gentle back and forth, back and forth. It was my great-grandmother's rocking chair, once lost, then found and loved back to its present use and dignity.

The chair became a character in my life in third grade when I first visited my great-grandmother's house in Osseo, Minnesota. She had difficulty walking, so sometimes she used crutches to get around. My great-grandmother loved to sit in her rocker and watch Saturday night wrestling matches on her black-and-white television. She watched Verne Gagne, wearing his world championship belt, wrestle the Crusher, the Bruiser, Killer Kowalski, Haystacks Calhoun, and Jesse "The Body" Ventura. She would get all tangled up in her crutches as she twisted her own tiny body in the moves, positions, and headlocks she wanted the wrestlers to make on television, all the while rocking in her chair.

I hadn't seen the old rocker for years. After my mother died, I visited my grandparents regularly. My grandfather enjoyed showing me his auction finds, and one day I noticed the rocker in the back of an old shed. It sat neglected, having been painted lime green in the 1950s, no doubt by a family member trying to make it fashionable. The upholstery was gone, revealing the horsehair padding beneath. It leaned to the side because the rockers had rotted on the damp shed floor. I had to climb over old cream cans and a trunk to get to it. It looked sad and abandoned, but I pulled out a house key and scraped the arm, removing the garish green paint to see traces of beautiful oak grain hidden beneath. This old chair had a natural beauty. Knowing it was the chair I remembered from my childhood was all I needed to drive back up to the farm a few weeks later to load it into the car and put in the investment and effort to resurrect it.

It was more than just a chair my grandfather had stored in the shed. The chair held pride and dignity. My grandfather offered it to me as a gift to say thank you for small checks I had sent my grandparents from time to time. With my mother gone, I had assumed her place in the family and tried to offer support to my grandparents in whatever small ways I could. This sweet old rocking chair, sorely in need of repair, was an offering of gratitude from my grandfather to me—and to my mother in spirit.

When I took the chair, I wasn't aware that my great-grandmother had also played a part in Lila's story. I later learned that she helped my grandfather with a gift of twenty-five hundred dollars toward Lila's bail. That was a lot of money to an older woman living alone in her modest house in 1959. She gave it because that's what one does for family.

Looking at my grandson's sweet, sleeping tiny face, I feel this chair filled with family history holding the two of us. I am mindful of how our ancestors hold us when we need to be held. They hold us especially when we have hard work to do. They hold us when we are opening their secrets, secrets they carried for too many years, stories they don't have to carry any longer now they're gone. They hold us as we tell their stories. These stories weighed down my grandparents, my mother, and Lila as they left this life. It is time to set their stories free.

Today, my surviving relatives—the living ancestors—hold the stories, and they have been generous in the telling. Who knows? Perhaps it has set them free as well, so they can lay down their heavy memories and walk lighter to the end of their own lives. They trusted me and anointed me with their tears, prayers, laughter, and blessings to write it, all of it. My uncle Sidney said, "We're so glad you're telling this story."

As I rock quietly with Liam in my arms, I'm grateful to be sitting in this chair remembering. Someday he may sit in this chair rocking his own baby, reading Lila's story and his great-grandmother's story and marveling at the strength and courage of his ancestors. I hope he will be proud that his own grandmother wrote this story, healed because of it, and cleared the path for him to make his own way, his own life, unencumbered by anything other than what being human has to deliver.

# 25

## Sleep in Heavenly Peace

### *2014*

The scent of pine and burning candles floats in the air of the church sanctuary. Garlands of green drape across the dark oak railing in front of the pulpit, lit by tiny twinkling lights mirroring the soft glow of two wreaths above the choir loft. Deep red and white poinsettias crowd each other for attention, donated remembrances of loved ones lost or celebrations honored. We placed one there this year to celebrate our grandson's exceptional baptism in this church that dedicates infants. At the baptism service, our thoughtful minister, Reverend Travis Norvell asked the congregation, "When do we begin to grow saints?" He opened his pastoral heart to our family as he extended this ritual outside our tradition.

"Silent night, holy night." The familiar refrain rises to the rafters, caressing and blessing this space as the lights go out and we are all held in darkness. The Christ candle from the Advent wreath is used to light the first candle as we stand in the dark, circling the sanctuary, each of us holding a candle, preparing to pass the light from one to another, waiting for our own candlelight to brighten the dark.

My eyes rise to witness the beauty around me, and I give thanks to Harry Wild Jones, the architect who designed this sanctuary over one hundred years ago. He created more than just a space for worship: it is a true sanctuary for those who desire a place to question, to feel included and welcomed no matter who they are and the wounds they bring with them. This became a place to strive for justice and equity for all. As I look around the circle at my friends, I see former Lutherans, Catholics, and Episcopalians, and a few random Baptists. The beautiful stained glass windows are darkened by the night sky, wrapping us in a blanket of comfort for this one night as we all feel anticipation and a little promise of new life, no matter the questions of yesterday.

"All is calm, all is bright." The candlelight passes from one person to another, encircling half the sanctuary, lighting the faces of women standing with their wives; men standing with their husbands; Black, white, and Asian faces; grandmother and grandfather faces; faces touched by cancer, stroke, trauma, and death this past year. Each face is lined with its own story.

"Round yon virgin, mother and child, holy infant so tender and mild." The candlelight approaches as I look to my right and see Ryan, my tall, muscular son-in-law, holding tiny eight-month-old Liam in his arms while lighting the candle in my daughter's hand, the new holy trinity in our lives joining us in this circle this Christmas Eve. I feel so grateful that my daughter has such a good man to share her life. The song now becomes a hum as the candlelight is passed within my family, to my husband, Willie, on this, our forty-seventh Christmas Eve together, then to Zack, our son, who flew home from New York City to be with us for the holidays. Like his father, he is a thoughtful and principled man. The golden candlelight on these dear faces is the hearth where I now warm my life.

As the flame is passed to me, I am aware that I have stood in this candlelight with sorrow in my heart for years, but this year is different. I arrived in this sanctuary almost forty years ago, after my mother died in her sleep during the holiday season, and every year, on Christmas Eve, I have grieved her absence. Sudden shocking loss takes so long to heal. As I look into Liam's little Korean-Irish face, look into the sweet faces of my family, watch the final candle close the circle rounding the entire sanctuary, I feel the last small opening of the unhealed hole in my heart close over and feel peace. We stand in this circle of families and friends and sing ourselves to quiet as we blow out the candles. Here we are beckoning hope as we stand in the darkness, held together by something greater than ourselves. "Sleep in heavenly peace, sleep in heavenly peace."

# 26

## Amen

In 1959, when my aunt Lila shot and killed her husband, women's rights and domestic violence weren't even on the radar. It was long before Betty Friedan and Gloria Steinem wrote the treatises that inspired women to reach beyond the roles to which they had been consigned. The not-guilty verdict that Lila received was nothing short of a miracle. It remains a miracle today, as women continue to be sent to prison for defending themselves and their children against men trying to kill them, when murder seems the only way out.

Box 136, Little Pine Route was the address of my grandparents' farm. Today, the mailbox stands on the dirt road, its flag rusted in the down position, indicating there is no mail to be picked up, no letters telling of daily chores, the weather, the Watkins man's visit, a death in the family, or neighbors dropping in. Folks who drive by see an old mailbox, but this farm holds our family's history. The white clump birch greeted us as we drove the road into the farm, along the marsh where the spring peepers sang us home as we returned from town or a nearby hayfield or berry picking in the woods.

The house my grandfather built sits on the rise overlooking the pastures. I am sure he was pleased the day he moved his family upstairs, out of the basement, into a home he built with his own hands. My grandmother put up café-style curtains in the kitchen and bought a nylon frieze sofa for the living room. The counter where my grandmother's crockery bowl sat, holding the sourdough starter covered with a pie tin, now gathers dust. They bought their first electric stove, where the pancake griddle was immediately placed, but delicious odors no longer waft through the house. The Formica-topped table where many family suppers were served is now gone.

The outhouse still stands on the hill, over the rise, weathered and gray, a testament to modernity in its time (two holes instead of one), the Sears and Roebuck catalog resting on the board in between. The garage is still there: the magical place where my grandfather repaired engines, welded broken parts, and built sawmills. There are no sounds of motors running, saws humming, or hammers pounding. Today the barn houses mostly barn swallows, field mice, and occasional critters taking shelter from winter winds. The sheds are empty of tools and the numerous treasures my grandfather found at farm auctions.

My grandparents were the hub of the wheel that turned family life on the farm. As the years crawled by, the spokes of their wheel spun out into the world, with their children returning to the farm only for holidays, deer hunting, or to help with haying season.

My mother was the first of my grandparents' children to die. Losing their oldest child, the one who bore many responsibilities and had been a tremendous support during difficult times in the family, was a devastating loss. I do believe it broke my grandfather's heart, literally. I didn't dare tell my grandparents that my mother's ashes were scattered on the farm, or they never would have sold it. When my grandfather died, my grandmother, along with my uncle Dale, moved to the town of Crosby. This placed them close to the clinic, the pharmacy, the funeral parlor, and the church. After my grandmother's death in 1995, her funeral was held at the Methodist church between Crosby and Deerwood. Knowing it would be too painful, I didn't want to officiate her funeral, but I did share these words at her service: "I grew to have a relationship with God. My life has been inspired by Jesus, but the Holy Spirit has always eluded me until recently, when I realized that the Holy Spirit was like my grandmother—a dynamic loving grace that moved in, around, and among us, transforming all of us with her love." My grandparents now rest in the Emily cemetery north of Ross Lake Township.

Lila lived almost another fifty years after the trial. She rose from the ordeal and made a life for herself. It wasn't a perfect life. She married two more men; she outlived one of those husbands and not the other. She birthed a son with her second husband. At one point, after she married for the second time, she and her family moved in with my mother and me in our Minneapolis home, perhaps to escape the ever-present pall that hung over her past in a small community.

Some years later, she returned to her northern small town and spent the rest of her life there. She worked hard in the kind of jobs available for women in rural areas. Life wasn't easy. She made mistakes but continued to have a wry wit and a sparkle in her eye. Her resilience was extraordinary. As far as I know, she never suffered physical abuse again. She died on September 17, 2007.

During my years as a hospital chaplain, sometimes caring for patients who had been in abusive relationships, with each patient I felt as if I got a glimpse of what Lila endured. Physical violence slices through the skin and cuts down to the bone. I saw it with my own eyes. For these patients, surviving becomes a primal matter. Until men stand up to other men and demand that this expression of authority and entitlement stop, domestic violence will never end.

In the 1950s in rural Minnesota, there were no resources for a woman caught in the snare of a violent man. People often ask why women stay in abusive relationships. Research reveals they stay because they want to live and because they are trying to keep their children alive. In the 1950s there was no place to turn for help, no escape, no shelter. Some women didn't make it and died at the hands of their husbands and boyfriends. Even today, with more available resources, domestic homicide is too common.

For other women it is a different story, as it was for Lila. Each woman's experience is unique. She must weigh what is at stake and the risks involved in getting out. She must go to the worst possible outcome and then work her way back to what is realistic and safe for her and her children. Sometimes the situation is outside of her control, and a woman has to make that decision in an instant. That impulse can't always be deliberated. It becomes a matter of life and death. When her life and the lives of her children are at stake, an outsider can't imagine the hell in which she exists. Against every loving voice within, against every ounce of wishing it were different, against every legal implication, the frontal cortex of the brain fires a fight-or-flight signal, and the primal animal instinct to survive and save one's young takes over.

I feel great sorrow that my aunt had to save herself and her baby with a shotgun. I feel great sorrow that my mother had to flee with me on a Greyhound bus. Children in such circumstances carry the effects of these experiences for the rest of their lives—as I have. The trauma can cut so deep that it wipes away spans of memory or takes deep therapy to heal. Today there are years of distance between these three choices: a shotgun, a bus, or therapy and writing.

Today three of the Palmer children are still living and reside in Brainerd. It has not been easy for my uncle Sidney and aunt Della to have these old memories stirred. Sidney has had remarkable recall of details and events. Della's voice still cracks if we venture in too deep. The two of them have been steadfast and patient in the face of my questions. When I offered to share what I have been writing, Della, with her usual spirit and humor, simply said, "You are the one doing all the work. You get to write it any way you want to." Sidney said, "It is a story that needs to be told." I could not have written this story without their love and support.

# The End of Wondering

## *2017–2018*

> When you don't have a father—or no; when your mother withholds from you who that father is—the one thing you have to imagine is that he doesn't know you exist. She kept it from him, too, and that's not his fault! How could he know any better? But you figure he's got to find out—or one day when you're grown up, you'll find him. You'll know how.
>
> —Julia Glass, *And the Dark Sacred Night*

I was seventy-one years old when I found my father. I finally knew how. I like to believe that if my mother had known she was going to die at a young age, we would have had this important exchange of information as two adult women. We never had the chance.

I understand a woman withholding information, exercising one of her few weapons of power and resistance. It might happen after a young woman's heart is broken, when her engagement morphs into betrayal, promises cast aside, and dreams lost. On February 12, 1946, I was born, and the dawn of my wondering began as my mother made choices and kept secrets.

At age twenty-nine, when I first learned about my birth father, I began to come to terms with a lifetime of sadness and anger. After years of self-examination, I now see how believing my father didn't care enough to find me fueled anger and indignation that caused me to live a driven life. It spawned determination to stand up to men, insist I be taken seriously, and demand my right to a seat at the table. I wasn't going to tolerate mistreatment by men or male fools. I spent years attempting to fill the black hole of being a fatherless daughter in ways that did not lead to trust or healthy relationships.

But the truth was that my father didn't know I existed. He had been denied the truth by my mother, as had I. After the discovery of my father's identity, years intervened, filled with grief over the loss of my mother, work, marriage, infertility, adopting children, parenting, and seminary. I was too busy to dwell on him. Frankly, I didn't believe he had much to do with who I was. Contact with him might only complicate my life.

Then I watched my children be brave. When Kate and Zack were in college, my husband and I proposed we take a family trip to Korea. Both kids were ambivalent. I understood ambivalence, not wanting to rattle your world, settling for what is known, not feeling fully compelled to struggle to learn what is not known. Kate and Zack both had to sign a form from Children's Home Society to indicate if they wanted to do a birth family search. Eventually they both signed the form, and we made the journey, uncertain about what we might learn but certain we might be transformed in ways unknown to us.

On that trip, we witnessed our daughter meeting her foster mother, sisters, and nieces, the family that cared for her as a newborn baby. Kate was their first foster child, and they bonded with her so intimately that relinquishing her was too painful, and they never fostered a baby again. Kate learned how much she meant to this family in their emotional reunion. Attempts to contact Kate's birth mother were unsuccessful. We learned that many Korean women have to hide their previous pregnancies or men will not marry them. Kate's birth mother is most likely now married with a family. Our daughter is a secret she must keep in a treasured corner of her heart. To meet Kate would be too great a risk. I told Kate I was sorry she did not have the opportunity to meet her mother. Her response was, "If I weren't as happy as I am with you and Dad, then it would be more important."

The attempts to reach Zack's family were also unsuccessful at first. Then, suddenly, the social worker informed us that Zack's family had responded and wanted to meet him. We later learned that Zack was the youngest of five children born into a poor rural family. The father in the family was very ill, and they could not afford another child. The mother had her brother drive her to another village to give birth, unbeknownst to her other children. Zack was born prematurely, and they did not know he had survived. We supported Zack through a very emotional reunion with his birth mother, father, two brothers, and two sisters.

His mother wailed in Korean, "We are so sorry! We are so sorry!" Zack's birth mother's sorrow and regret echoed off the walls in that room as she clung to him. Then she turned and embraced me, one mother holding another, sobbing and saying, "Thank you, thank you." The overwhelming joy and gratitude in that reunion was the beginning of healing many losses. Zack's birth family embraced not only him but also Kate when they learned she had not found her birth mother.

As I watched my children risk knowing more about themselves, I felt the visceral power of ending the wondering, finding pieces of oneself and one's identity. My daughter taught me it is okay to not find all the answers because the life we live together is so blessed. Her gifts and potential go beyond one piece of information. She has the love, foundation, and tools to build her own life well and create her own family. And who knows? In years to come a birth mother's life may change, a space may open, and she may turn her heart west. We can't imagine the circumstances or the heart of a mother halfway around the world. But waiting is keeping faith in its own way.

My son taught me that it is possible to fill in large pieces in the puzzle of our identity, but it does not alter the whole of your life. It just adds more chapters to your story, more substance and content as you grow up. He now has less wondering.

My friend Charlie once told me, "Conversation with a dear friend is akin to prayer." A prayer I didn't even know was on my heart was answered when I had a conversation with my friend Lee over lunch. Lee had been adopted by a Minnesota family at the end of World War II but knew his birth family was on the West Coast. For his seventieth birthday gift to himself, he decided to do a birth family search using a court intermediary in Seattle. Over lunch, he told me and my husband the story of finding his birth family and meeting his half-brother for the first time. It was a powerful recollection. At the end of lunch, something moved me to ask for the intermediary's contact information.

One day soon thereafter, I was reading Julia Glass's novel *And the Dark Sacred Night*, and during a quiet moment my mind drifted to this contact, so I sent an email. I shared the only three facts I had about my father: his name, Joseph Hyder; that he had worked in a military hospital in Vancouver, Washington; and that he drove a convertible. My mother's friend Fern had double-dated with Joe and my mother in that convertible. It seemed a funny fact on a serious search, but it turned out to be an important detail. After the court intermediary received my email, she asked me to call her right away, and we discussed my search.

Three days later, the intermediary called me and said, "I just got off the telephone with your uncle." Her news felt surreal. I had a rush of emotions. I learned my father was the oldest of four children and was now deceased. This was not surprising, since he would have been ninety-eight years old. His youngest brother, John, was eighty-eight and the only one of four siblings still living. When the intermediary reached John, she explained she was conducting a birth family search for a woman in Minnesota and posed three questions to him.

"Are you the brother of Joe Hyder?" Yes, he was. "Did your brother work in a military hospital during the war?" John replied enthusiastically, "Yes, he worked in the Barnes General Hospital in Vancouver, Washington. He made glasses for soldiers during the war." Then she asked if Joe drove a convertible. "Yes, yes, he drove a convertible. I was sixteen and so impressed with his convertible. He was ten years older than I was, and I loved that car."

The intermediary informed him that his brother had fathered a daughter, so he had a niece. Then he said, "I'm so excited. I have to get off the telephone and tell my wife. I have some photos I can send this woman so she can see what her father looked like."

In her search, the intermediary had discovered other information. She asked John one more question. "Did Joe have two daughters?"

"Yes, he did, and I have contact with one of them." That day I learned I have two half-sisters.

The next day I received an email with an attachment. I looked at the little box and held the cursor over it for a moment. My wondering was about to end. I was about to see the last hidden puzzle piece of my own life story. I moved the cursor to the tiny box and clicked. A black-and-white photo opened, and there was his face.

*There you are. I found you. I am seventy-one years old and looking at a photograph of you for the first time in my life. You look like a nice man, a decent sort, a good citizen. Your face is kind. This is important to me. I was hoping you wouldn't look like a man who had lived hard. You could be my next-door neighbor.*

Fern had told me that I really looked like my father. Like a mother looking at a newborn baby for the first time, I searched for traces of myself. I saw myself in his cheekbones and jawline. *Brown hair, yes. Brown eyes, yes. Your eyelids, my eyelids—until I had mine corrected to improve my vision. We have similar noses, though my mother had a knobby nose too. Lips, not sure, though I don't have my mother's mouth.* My eyes filled with tears. *Yes, I am your daughter.*

How different might our lives have been had we known about one another? Perhaps the living of our lives would have remained the same, but we each would, at least, have known the other was walking around in the world. I thought about what I had missed, what we had missed.

I was tentative about connecting with the family at first. I sent a letter to the intermediary to be forwarded to them, explaining who I was, why I was searching at that time in my life. John and I eventually connected through email and became active correspondents. He was smart, computer savvy, generous with information, had a great sense of humor, and, ironically, was the family genealogist. He was thrilled to discover another family member.

I learned more from John about my two half-sisters, one two years younger and one five years younger than I am. He indicated that my youngest sister might be in touch with me at some point. We all needed time to catch up with this new development in our lives. Once the correspondence with my sister Lynn began, there was no doubt that I wanted to meet the family, so in the fall of 2018 my husband and I traveled to Portland, Oregon.

As we stepped off the elevator in our hotel, we met a handsome man and a lovely woman with a beautiful smile who resembled me. We embraced.

All I could say was "Thank you." The four of us immediately felt at ease, walked to a nearby restaurant, and talked for several hours over dinner and wine. My sister and I learned that the trajectories of our lives were a bit different, but we had many of the same values and strong family ties. Lynn shared truths about our father, who had been an army medic in the South Pacific during the war. Many men never talked about their horrific war experiences, instead dealing with it silently at the expense of their health. I learned that even a father who is present can be absent.

Our time together exceeded any hopes I could have had for this meeting. In our holiday letters to friends and family that year, my sister and I each shared our joy at finding each other. We remain in touch, getting to know one another, filling in parts of the story, adding in pieces of the puzzle. In her recent note, she signed off, "Time for bed, sister."

Willie and I then traveled to Florence, Oregon, to meet my uncle John, the one who made all of it possible. He was now ninety years old, living with his wife, Lila. The coincidence of her name did not escape us. They picked us up at our hotel and drove us along the coast to a beautiful restaurant right on the Pacific Ocean. We shared more stories and laughs and got to know one another. They invited us back to their home for dessert, where we looked at family photographs, Lila's needlework, and John's handmade Charlie Brown Christmas trees. In a quiet moment, Lila said, "When the contact first came, I asked John, what if she is a con artist?" We laughed and exchanged our cautionary tales of tiptoeing into this contact with one another. Their warm hospitality and generosity—as family once lost, now found—held such love. Henri Amiel's quote about "keeping a space in your heart for the unexpected guest" comes to mind. John and Lila, and Lynn and Lee, surely did that.

As I write these closing words, one of John's handmade Christmas trees stands in my window, lighting my way into the coming year with bright colors and a springy yellow star on top, reminding me of many blessings of this past year. I've exchanged more loving letters by email with John and Lynn.

John O'Donohue wrote in *Eternal Echoes: Celtic Reflections on Our Yearning to Belong*, "Ideally, a human life is a constant pilgrimage of discovery. The most exciting discoveries happen at the frontiers. When you come to know something new, you come closer to yourself and the world." As a child, I was powerless to influence my mother's mischances, sorrows, and choices, so they became mine as well. Still, as Mary Oliver says, I had alleviations and blessings throughout my life that healed those raw places. At this time in my life, I want to be brave, the way my children were brave, so I have written this story. It has helped me heal and get closer to myself. I also traveled west and reached out my hand, and these strangers welcomed me. They helped me take one more step toward knowing myself and the world. Through grace, my life has continued to be a constant pilgrimage of discovery.

# Acknowledgments

A personal story gets written with the support of angels and cheerleaders. Nine years ago, a woman named Allyn Timmons asked a single question and opened the door to this story. I walked through and could not turn back. Thank you for that grace-filled question, Allyn.

A meeting with my Aunt Della and Uncle Sidney ended with Sidney's words: "It is a story that needs to be told," so I did. I could not have written this story without your help and blessing. I pray you and others in this story understand that I needed to write it from my experience, but with a deep desire to honor my family and all it has meant to me.

Thank you to the Minnesota History Center, the Crow Wing County Historical Society, Attorney Tom Fitzpatrick, and Jim Ryan, who provided important details.

Sincere gratitude to Paula Moyer and Sara Evans for their willingness to read the worst first drafts of this story, yet encouraged me to keep writing. Patricia Weaver Francisco, through the Loft Manuscript Coaching and Critiquing Program, gave me the confidence I needed to believe this was an important story. Editor Sarah Howard provided her professional skills and important feedback. Beth Wright helped me place this story between two covers. She is the talented conductor of an orchestra of creative resources to help individuals self-publish. Thank you to all of you for helping me cross the finish line.

Another blessing was the urging and support of the "Writing as a Tool for Healing" class led by Patricia Hoolihan. Darcy, Jane, Laurie,

Margaret, Nanci, Judy, Kris U., Kris B., Sky, and Maria, thank you for your ongoing encouragement. You witnessed firsthand the tears shed as I attempted to birth this story. The Oberholtzer Foundation and Mallard Island provided the perfect retreat and healing place to finish writing this story. In addition, thank you to dear friends—you know who you are— who believed in me and called this a book before I dared to imagine it.

Words can't adequately express my deep respect, admiration, and gratitude to Suzy Whelan, former director of SafeJourney, and Dr. Mark Berg, former Emergency Department physician at North Memorial Health Care. They both worked in the trenches with women and men who suffered domestic abuse. They continued to tell me this was a powerful story and to keep going. I pray I have executed it well.

My spiritual community, Judson Church, loved me into a place where I could even begin to consider writing this story. This church accepted me where I was, not where the church expected me to be. I am eternally grateful to Walt, Dale, and Travis, who encouraged us to understand we are all ministers.

My children, Kate and Zack: you were my reasons to seek healing. Being your mother has been my utter joy. Son-in-law Ryan: you have expanded our family in many loving ways—most important, loving us, our daughter, and our grandchildren gently. I hope this story helps my grandchildren, Liam and Stella, know their Gam a bit better and pieces of their family history. They are sweet, loving lights in these later years of my life.

Living with a woman with my history can be complicated. For over fifty years, Willie has been my constant, loving foundation. Together we have created a life I never could have imagined when I was a little girl. I love you dearly and give thanks for you each and every day.

# Sources

*Brainerd [Minnesota] Daily Dispatch.* July and November 1959.

Buechner, Frederick. *The Sacred Journey: A Memoir of Early Days.* New York: Harper & Row, 1982.

Day, Dorothy. *The Long Loneliness.* New York: Harper & Brothers, 1952.

Hillesum, Etty. *An Interrupted Life: The Diaries 1941–1943.* Translated by Arnold J. Pomerans. New York: Henry Holt, 1996.

O'Donohue, John. *Eternal Echoes: Celtic Reflections on Our Yearning to Belong.* New York: Harper Collins, 1998.

Oliver, Mary. *Upstream: Selected Essays.* New York: Random House, 2016.

Shriver, Maria. "Maria Shriver Interviews the Famously Private Poet Mary Oliver." *O Magazine.* March 9, 2011.

# Resources

*Minnesota*
Casa de Esperanza Bilingual Domestic Violence Helpline
651-772-1611

MN Day One Crisis Line
866-223-1111

OutFront Minnesota LGBTQ Anti-Violence Crisis Line
800-800-0350

*National*
National Domestic Violence Hotline
800-799-7233
TTY 800-787-3224

National Deaf Domestic Violence Hotline
Video phone: 855-812-1001
nationaldeafhotline@adwas.org

StrongHearts Native American Domestic Violence Helpline
844-762-8483

What to expect if you call a hotline:
- direct contact to domestic violence programs near you
- help with finding resources in your area, including shelters, counseling, legal assistance, and advocacy
- crisis assistance, emotional support, and safety planning
- access to advocates in many languages
- confidentiality

CPSIA information can be obtained
at www.ICGtesting.com
Printed in the USA
LVHW020047060821
694500LV00012B/781